NURTURING NEW FAMILIES

NURtURINg NeW FamilieS

A guide to supporting parents and their newborn babies

Naomi Kemeny

Nurturing New Families:
a guide to supporting parents and their newborn babies

First published in Great Britain by Pinter & Martin Ltd 2014

© 2014 Naomi Kemeny

Naomi Kemeny has asserted her moral right to be identified as the author of this work in accordance with the Copyright, Designs and Patents Act of 1988.

ISBN 978-1-78066-165-0

British Library Cataloguing-in-Publication Data
A catalogue record for this book is available from the British Library.

Editor Susan Last

Index Helen Bilton

Set in Minion & Verlag

Printed and bound in the UK by TJ International Ltd, Padstow, Cornwall

This book has been printed on paper that is sourced and harvested from sustainable forests and is FSC accredited.

Pinter & Martin Ltd
6 Effra Parade
London SW2 1PS

www.pinterandmartin.com

CONTENTS

POEM OF DEDICATION

It is you who care
You who listen.
It is you who guide
You who support.
It is you who observe
But never judge.
It is you who do
But never overdo.
It is you who are there
But know when to step back.
It is you who are privileged
Never complacent.
It is you who arrive
And you who know
When it is time for farewell…

Naomi Kemeny

INTRODUCTION
How I became a postnatal doula

My earliest memory of wanting to be with babies was when I was about ten years old. This was in the times when fears of being out on the street did not ruin our childhood and babies were parked outside shops gurgling. I offered to do an errand for our neighbour, Bunty. She asked me to take her baby for a walk in her pram and collect something from the chemist. (I now realise that she was just desperate for a break!). I remember feeling so excited and proud to be given that responsibility. Not quite grasping the concept of money, I decided it would be nice to buy Bunty a present (think, early pampering instinct!), so I bought a pretty soap with her money and gave it to her on my return. She must have thought I was a bit crazy but thanked me graciously for my gift.

Next came kittens… I spent hours in the airing cupboard watching these tiny mites, overwhelmed by their cuteness. Then came dolls. I would take in my friends' dolls and make them tiny outfits.

As a new mother myself I took in several 'homeless' friends with new babies. I stayed with friends in need to help with their babies, caring and cooking for them.

The first birth apart from my own (hospital, home, home) that I attended was to support a single mum friend and it is one I will never forget. The midwife at the home birth said 'You could do this, you know'. I'd never thought of being a midwife. These words always stayed with me.

Later a friend told me she was an auxiliary nurse on our

local hospital maternity ward. She described how she saw all the births and helped with the babies. Well, that was it for me: I went straight for it and loved it.

Several years on I started to feel I wanted more responsibility and although I never imagined I would, or even could, as I was not academic, I applied to train as a midwife and got a place against all odds. It was a huge achievement to qualify and to this day I never regret the time and energy I dedicated to becoming a midwife. I delivered many babies and rotated through all areas of maternity care.

However, during this time I was also mum to a toddler and two teenagers. It was a very stressful and exhausting time. My personal situation then changed. My mother-in-law came to live with us following a stroke and I got ME. Eventually I knew I had to make a choice and something had to go. Sadly it was midwifery.

Time heals and I gradually regained my strength and confidence, through working as a school nurse for four and a half years. During this time I also volunteered for Homestart (a charity that supports families), which was an invaluable experience.

I remember how I missed working with babies so much, but I always believed there would be a way back for me. In fact I even designed the words for a leaflet to market myself years before I'd even heard of doulas. When I learned that doulas existed it was decision time! I would do postnatal doula training and get started.

I was clear from the start that I only wanted to do postnatal work. Although I know it is an incredible experience to support a woman through labour and witness the miracle and joy of birth, I felt, that as a midwife, I had had my fill of hospital stress with too many emergency Caesareans and overstretched staff. However, I never closed the door completely and decided to do the birth doula section of the course 'just in case'! I then took on a hardship case single mum. I have no regrets in doing this and thankfully the outcome was positive. It was a wonderful home birth with just me attending until the midwives and ambulance crew finally turned up twenty minutes before delivery! This experience was invaluable in that it renewed my confidence and showed me that I could and did cope well. It was healing and incredible, but at the moment I don't attend births. I personally prefer not to be on call and do enjoy the security of postnatal hours. One of the most satisfying things to see during my time with new mothers is the striking changes that take place over the weeks.

New mums start off exhausted and are often struggling in this sensitive time of transition. My support, help and suggestions are always readily accepted. On a day-to-day basis I am providing emotional support by being there to listen, comfort and chat. On a practical level I am there to ensure she is drinking, eating and resting and therefore regaining her strength. I also fold a lot of laundry and empty a lot of dishwashers and play with a lot of toddlers! I am quite happy to do this, but honestly? The best bit is cuddling and caring for the baby, knowing that mum can have a rest. It is very reassuring when I leave, seeing mums back on their feet and feeling more confident about coping in their new role. I also love to see how tiny newborn babies grow into babies that are kicking and smiling at me when I leave.

I know now that all the threads of my maternity experiences have connected, giving me a most rewarding career. I absolutely love being a postnatal doula. It rarely feels like work; I am more like a very privileged but paid grandmother! In all my working life I have never felt so appreciated and I look forward to many more jobs ahead.

> '... playing the doula is one of those few experiences in life when answering someone's deep need can offer the giver an equal reward...'
>
> Dana Raphael

CHAPTER 1
What is postnatal support?

If you have chosen this book then you must be planning to support a new mother and her baby during the early postnatal period. Or you may be a mother-to-be curious about the support and care you might need, and wondering who will provide it. Whoever you are: mother-to-be, partner, mother, sister, friend or postnatal doula, you know that a new mother deserves the best quality of care. To provide this focussed loving care is a *gift* to any new family, one which will affect their personal journey throughout parenthood.

Traditionally in many countries the 'lying-in' period has been respected and held to be of great importance. It is a crucial time for cherishing and caring for the new mother and baby. Virtually every country that maintains this tradition will support newly delivered mothers by creating a warm sense of community, with female relations and friends providing nourishing foods and the opportunity for the mother to rest and recuperate following delivery. Sadly this practice has been lost in the West and many women feel pressured, thanks to the expectations of society, to be 'up and about' too quickly. Although well prepared for birth, they are often ill prepared for the challenges of the reality of the postnatal period.

We need to recreate this lying-in period through our supportive presence and 'mother the mother', both emotionally and physically. The mother is not an invalid needing to stay in bed, but a healthy woman who has just been through the monumental feat and incredible achievement of childbirth and now needs the opportunity to rest, be restored and enjoy nurturing and bonding with her new baby.

Some women who are planning to help their friends or relations with their new baby may not actually have had any hands-on experience themselves. Even if you have had your own babies, no one else's situation will ever be exactly the same. Each mother and baby is unique. Their needs will be dictated by their individual physical and mental characteristics.

My aim is to provide an informal, informative and inspirational tool, to be used as guidance for you either as a 'lay' carer offering postnatal support, or as a postnatal doula. The information provided in this book aims to distil all the information 'out there' into a user-friendly form. The ideas and suggestions cover all the important aspects of practical and emotional care needed during the postnatal period.

The information and tips are drawn from my personal experience, and there are contributions from other doulas. I found it hard to 'finish' the book because, as a practising postnatal doula, I am continually learning and experiencing more. This will, I hope, be the same for you.

I became motivated to write this book when I became an assessor/mentor for trainee doulas and realised that there was a lack of written information on the subject. Many doulas, despite having been on a doula training course, would still approach me wanting more information about what the job truly entails. Thus I felt compelled to write about and share the experience, knowledge and tips that I have gained from the many varied jobs that I have had over the years. If you are thinking of becoming a professional postnatal doula then the section on that subject will give you all the information that you will need; if you are considering providing support to a friend or relative you will also find a wide range of relevant and helpful information.

Whilst I was writing the book I had a lot of positive interest from friends and clients, and clients' relatives, who would ask me for my tips and recipes. It soon became clear that the book could be valuable for anyone planning to look after new mothers.

There are countless books on caring for newborns, but the mother (and the rest of the family) is usually left out of the picture. This guide gives valuable suggestions on all practical and (holistic) emotional issues to do with caring for and supporting the new mother, her family *and* her baby (or babies!).

If you are reading this book then I believe you truly care and want to make a difference. You are keen to expand your knowledge and this will improve your ability to help. By arming yourself with the information in this book you will undoubtedly contribute to improving women's overall experiences during this precious time in their lives.

The positive effects of good postnatal care ripple outwards: anyone receiving your gift of care will know how good it feels and hopefully, in time, they will be able to provide the same support for their own friends, family and future grandchildren.

NB: Of course, the primary carers of new mothers are her midwife, doctor and health visitor. For the purposes of simplicity and clarity I will refer to women as mothers and fathers/partners as partners.

'The postnatal period begins immediately after birth and extends for about six weeks. It is a time when the mother's body, including hormone levels and uterus size, returns to how it was before pregnancy. The newborn infant also starts to adapt to life outside the womb and its health during this time will be monitored. This time is also referred to as the puerperium.'[*]

---

[*] See **drfosterhealth.co.uk/medical-dictionary/maternity/postnatal.aspx**

Why is there a need for postnatal support?

Once discharged from hospital a new mother will be under the care of a midwife for a minimum of ten days. She will then meet her health visitor, who will support her until her child is five years old. A health visitor offers parents support and advice on family health, carries out regular development reviews and may arrange vaccinations or referrals to other healthcare professionals. She will also provide families with specific support on subjects such as weaning or postnatal depression. This necessary basic postnatal support is vastly different from the traditional lying-in period mentioned above.

'Never in history were a mother and a father expected to care for their baby all by themselves. The idea of a nuclear family – one mother and one father to do it all – is one of mankind's most recent, and riskiest, experiments, attempted only over the last two or three generations...' Karp (2002). In an ideal situation the extended family would be able to provide continuous support at this early stage of parenting. The modern family is all too often nuclear and separate from the local community network, unlike in many traditional communities worldwide, where they live more in line with the old African proverb, 'It takes a village to raise a child'. Therefore many new mothers find themselves isolated and lacking support.

Holland is the only country that provides an overall free package of postnatal care to all new families. Trained maternity assistants are provided for up to ten days, giving practical support in the home, helping with other children, cooking, tidying and providing feeding support, very similar to a doula. 'Picture a cross between the Fairy Godmother and Mary Poppins and the result might just be a *kraamzorg*, a trained healthcare professional that helps new mothers in the Netherlands in the first few days after a birth.'*

> Post-natal depression is prevalent in our society, occurring in 10 to 15 per cent of new mothers.

---

* See **wavetrust.org/intervention/details/kraamzorg-postnatal-service-netherlands**

> Many families nowadays are dispersed. Due to the current economic climate, with jobs being harder to get, families may be forced to move away from their friends and relatives to take whatever job they can, however far afield.

> New mothers are discharged much earlier from hospital than in the past. This can be within six hours of a normal delivery and as little as one night after a caesarean section. This means that some women feel they have not received adequate help prior to leaving hospital with issues such as feeding or handling the baby.

> Unfortunately, due to tight NHS budgets new mothers may not get the midwifery support that they need at home. A report from the National Federation of Women's Institutes (NFWI) and the National Childbirth Trust (NCT) (*Support Overdue: Women's Experiences of Maternity Services,* 2013) showed that the vast majority of maternity units have to cope with shortages of midwives. Almost two-thirds of new mothers feel let down by the NHS after giving birth, and their care varies according to where they live. In some areas mothers get three home visits after birth, whereas in others they may get only one. Sixty per cent of women wanted more support with postnatal care. Ruth Bond, chairman of the NFWI, said:

> 'Evidence shows that providing the right care and support in the transition to parenthood can have a long-term impact on the health and wellbeing of women and their families, yet women are being routinely failed, often this seems to be because of staff shortages'.

> Sadly some new mothers' own mothers are not there for them. Women may have a poor relationship history with their own mothers and not wish to have them present, or have suffered an early bereavement. Women today are having babies later in life, which can mean that their own mothers are older and not able, or available,

WHAT IS POSTNATAL SUPPORT?

to provide support. It's also the case that many modern grandparents are enjoying better health for longer and may struggle to find time and space in their own active lives to devote long periods of time to supporting their children and grandchildren.

> There is an increasing number of single parents and women choosing to 'go it alone'.

'There are few societies in which a single adult is responsible for the care of her babies and other children.' Romm (2002:61)

> Parents often have no previous experience of newborn babies until they are holding their own. This can be an unsettling and at times frightening experience, creating feelings of isolation and lack of confidence.

Who may need postnatal support?

Any mother! Mothers of all races and religions, single mothers, older mothers, teenage mothers, mothers of multiples, mothers with special needs, mothers with mental or physical health issues, mothers of babies with disabilities, same-sex parents, mothers who have had caesarean sections and normal deliveries, wealthy mothers, poverty-stricken mothers, mothers who have no family support, mothers

'There is a lot of help and support at the antenatal stage but very little after the baby is born and nothing that teaches you how to actually manage looking after a newborn. As my pregnancy neared its end, this gap in our knowledge was looming very large and becoming more and more alarming. I remembered the information I had read about doulas and, after discussing it with my husband and father, we all agreed that booking a doula for a few weeks would help us a lot.'

with family support, first-time mothers, mothers with lots of children, mothers who have suffered from postnatal depression, mothers who are suffering from birth trauma, mothers who have experienced bereavement at birth and mothers who have had hospital or home births...

Who can provide postnatal support?

1. Postnatal doula
2. Partner
3. Grandparent, Mother, Father
4. Friend

A new mother and her partner can feel vulnerable, exhausted and anxious in the days following birth. If so, they will need the presence of someone who has as many of the following qualities as possible – someone who is empathic, a good listener, can respect and uphold confidentiality, be sympathetic, non-judgmental, patient, has a sense of humour, be respectful, nurturing, caring, flexible, take initiative, prioritise activities, know when to refer for professional help, be able to respect personal boundaries, be confident in handling babies, be practical and able to prepare nourishing food, good with toddlers...

Don't worry if you don't yet feel you have all of these! This book will help to bring out these qualities in you so that you can provide effective support.

Postnatal doulas
What is a doula?

'Doula' is a Greek word meaning 'woman caregiver', 'handmaiden' or 'slave', or it can be loosely translated as 'in service of', but it has come to mean a woman who provides sustained physical and emotional support and information during labour and birth. A birth doula specialises in supporting women and their families through pregnancy, labour and birth. A postnatal doula provides similar support during the time immediately after birth and typically up to six weeks postpartum. This period is often referred to as the 'fourth trimester'. Some doulas may work in both areas.

Doulas are not medical professionals and do not perform clinical tasks, diagnose medical conditions, or give medical advice. There are currently around 1,000 doulas in the UK (2009, Doula UK).

A postnatal doula is there to 'mother the mother', *not* to provide professional or medical support.

My focus in this book is solely on the physical and emotional support that doulas can offer, not the business steps that need to be taken if you are setting up as a postnatal doula and marketing your services.

What does a postnatal doula do?

A postnatal doula is almost always a woman (although there is currently one male doula in Doula UK) who has been trained, assessed and recognised/qualified as a professional doula. Usually – but not always – they will have had children themselves. They offer practical and emotional support to newly delivered mothers. They usually meet the family before the birth to make sure both parties are compatible and comfortable with each other. They work flexible hours to suit the individual family's needs. They offer encouragement and suggestions as well as providing a supportive environment so that the mother can develop her own mothering skills in a relaxed and stress-free manner.

'Above all a postnatal doula is NOT there to tell the mother what to do. We should be there to encourage and inspire the mother to follow her inner maternal instinct. A shocking 82% of new mothers in a survey undertaken by BabyCalm state that they had received advice that went against their instinct.' *BabyCalm*, Sarah Ockwell-Smith (2012:14)

For a detailed list of a postnatal doula's daily activities, and in-depth practical tips, see Chapter 9.

Usually a postnatal doula will join a family soon after the birth for a period of six to eight weeks, although they

> 'I am generally wary of doing "too much" as I don't want to be indispensable. I see my role as, over time, making myself obsolete by showing the mummy how much she can do on her own.'

may sometimes be booked for 'emergency' help of just a few sessions. They may start immediately after the baby is born or sometimes once the partner has returned to work or a woman's mother or mother-in-law has left. They will work for a mutually agreed set number of hours per day, for up to several days a week.

It is in the mother's interest to have a doula for only the time that is deemed by both as beneficial and necessary. With experience a doula will know when it is time to go and leave the new mother to find her own way. In leaving the doula has the satisfaction of knowing that her job is done and the mother is 'good to go'.

> 'Postpartum doulas don't just answer questions, but actually show you how to care for your newborn. She's not there to hold the baby while you clean the house, though she'll certainly help with the baby if you want to rest, eat or shower. The postpartum doula's goal is to help you feel confident in caring for your baby.' Gurevich (2003)

The following are some ways in which a postnatal doula will provide support:

> She will give the mother space to discuss any concerns and issues and generally offers a source of information.
> Provide companionship.
> Give support with feeding choices/issues.
> She will know when to refer for professional help e.g. lactation consultant, GP.
> Offer assistance with caring for older children or the new baby, thus enabling the mother to rest.

'If I'd had time to think about it, I probably would have been nervous about someone intruding on our emotional space, but it was such a whirlwind during the time just before and after the birth of our triplets that it didn't occur to me to worry about the side effects of the extra help from our postnatal doula. The first day she arrived, we were still in bed after a torrid night of feeds, and it was a little bit embarrassing to think we might have kept her waiting while we got dressed so late in the day! But she immediately reassured us that we didn't have to "keep up appearances", and I began to relax very quickly.

Although the doula is supposed to be helping the mother of the child/children, this help clearly extended to me as the father and husband, especially since we had triplets. Also, feeling that my wife had this extra support and guidance meant there was a bit less pressure on me, and I discussed the minutiae of making formula and sleep deprivation with our doula almost as much as my wife did!

It was such a successful relationship that our doula ended up staying much longer than we had initially anticipated. By the last weeks of her involvement with us, I felt that she was not so much looking after my wife as looking after the whole family.'

> She can prepare food, do laundry and light housework, shopping, and help to maintain order within the home. Unlike a maternity nurse or nanny who tends to take over the care of the *baby*, a postnatal doula will assist the *mother* in her transition to motherhood and help her to find her own way in her new role.

> She will make it a priority that a new mother can catch up on sleep during her visit.

'I enjoyed my visits to R and N. Typically, on my arrival R and I would chat and a lovely trusting relationship developed. R was always organised with a prioritised list of things she needed help with. This was great for me as it meant I was sure of achieving what needed to be achieved, consequently I always left R at the end of my visit with a sense of satisfaction knowing that I had provided the best practical and emotional support possible in the time we had together. Some of the tasks I helped R with included picking tomatoes, collecting prescriptions, preparing food for R, tidying clothes away and caring for N so R could take a shower... and making chocolate chip cookies for everyone! What was so special, however, was that I held N in the car while R did a quick supermarket shop – the first time R had left N for any length of time! I felt so privileged that R had trusted me with this; I knew and understood what a huge step this was for her.'

> A doula is there to provide the mother with some time to herself, for example keeping an eye on the baby and/or other siblings whilst she takes a bath, shower or pops out for some fresh air. A Mumsnet survey found that mums say they are lucky to get half an hour to themselves each day, and 75 per cent say lack of me time is their major stress.

> The nature of a postnatal doula's work will vary greatly depending on whether this is the first baby or a mother with one or more children already. For a first-time mother more time is needed for the practical side of setting up equipment, bath demonstration, explaining use of slings and feeding support. If there are older siblings the doula may be required to spend more time with them.

The postnatal doula will also support and educate the father in his new role, as well as the mother. She can do this by demonstrating practical ways of supporting his partner.

Sometimes partners are not over-keen on someone else being there to help. It is therefore important to communicate equally with him and not exclude him. He may not be able to envisage what a postnatal doula will actually *do*. Once he sees things improving and that he has a calmer home life he will become more positive.

What are the advantages of having a postnatal doula?

'Every bit of help you receive adds to your reserves. Planning ahead for postpartum care ensures that you will have the help and support necessary to keep your well full.' Romm (2002)

With the help of a doula a woman can enjoy some of the benefits of a prolonged 'lying-in' period. She will then be

What does the mother need today?

able to avoid the pressure of rushing back in to normal day-to-day activities. She will be able to have time to bond with her baby and maintain her relationship with older siblings.

Evidence shows that postnatal doula support:

> Improves successful breastfeeding rates
> Reduces postnatal depression
> Eases the transition to parenthood
> Boosts confidence

How do parents find doulas?

Parents may find and contact doulas in a variety of ways:

> Via a 'find a doula' site on a doula website, i.e. Doula UK.
> Through a personal recommendation from a friend who has used a doula.
> They may have attended a doula talk or presentation.
> They may have picked up a leaflet or card from a Children's Centre.
> From adverts in parents' magazines or websites.
> They may have met postnatal doulas doing voluntary breastfeeding support in hospitals, baby clinics or breastfeeding cafés.
> Recommended by other health professionals.

How much does it cost?

Doulas are employed privately. Their charges vary depending on their experience, and trainee doulas charge a lot less. Cost can also vary depending on the geographical area. Friends and family can purchase and give doula gift vouchers (through Doula UK). This can be an enormously helpful gift to parents who can't afford to employ a doula themselves. Some clients say this gift of help is far more beneficial than endless baby clothes and unneeded toys and equipment.

Many doulas passionately believe that all new parents should have the opportunity to have their beneficial help during the postnatal period. They may offer to work with no charge and are reimbursed for their expenses from the Doula UK budget. Clients can apply through a doula access fund for this cost-free provision of care.

There are many doulas who give their time to volunteer in charity initiatives. For example **www.birthcompanions. org.uk** support vulnerable pregnant and newly delivered women in prison, and **www.hestia.org** support women subject to domestic violence.

Many doulas volunteer as breastfeeding supporters at Children's Centres, baby clinics, breastfeeding cafés and on hospital postnatal wards.

Doulas get their referrals in several ways:

> Recommendation from previous clients.
> Repeat bookings for second/ third babies.
> Private advertising, websites.
> Leaflet and card distribution in baby or children's venues.
> By meeting other mothers (clients' friends) whilst working.
> By networking with other local doulas who can recommend them if they are unable to take a job.

Being a postnatal doula

Much of the information below is relevant to *anyone* supporting new parents.

As a doula you will be entering a situation where a major life-changing event has just taken place, which will inevitably affect the family dynamic forever. We are offering ourselves as support at this time and in doing so our client's hopes and expectations are pinned on us. We have a huge responsibility in smoothing their transition to parenthood through our presence and by providing emotional and practical care. It is vital that we are sensitive and perceptive so that we can clearly anticipate the needs of our client. We need to empower the mother so that when things are going well she feels good. We must also be reassuring and encouraging when she is struggling. We may make suggestions, but must allow her to make her own decisions and implement her own plan.

Entering into the life of a new family can be daunting for the doula and family alike. Mothers may be initially shy, nervous, guarded and full of unanswered questions. It takes time for any relationship to develop and build, and become relaxed and trusting. This comes gradually from our commitment, consistent attendance to their needs, reading their signs, and taking their lead. It is also apparent that we are dealing with more than just the woman. We will enter into a new area of family relationships and dynamics. Partners, married couples, same sex families, single parents and wider extended families have an influence one way or another. There is always a wide range of relationships to encounter, from gushing mothers showering me with kisses and some grandmas feeling threatened and being quite cold and unfriendly. It is a delicate path we tread so as not to make new grandmothers feel overshadowed or intimidated. As a postnatal doula you are most likely to meet, and indeed be around, the 'new' grandparents. It is important from the start that they understand your role in their family's home. Hopefully your presence will have been explained and bring comfort and reassurance to them, not a threat.

Listening is one of the most important things a mother needs from us. There are often many complex emotional issues that come out after childbirth. It might take time for her to open up and she may never do this or need to. You may be the first person she unravels her birth experience with, whether positive or negative. Debriefing the birth experience could take up the entire first visit and may come up at any time during subsequent visits (always check that they have had this opportunity with their midwife and/or birth doula).

You will be presented with many practical concerns. Everything to do with the baby is described in graphic detail from the first skin blemish to full-blown baby acne. Descriptions of poos are from marmite to mustard and everything in between. Other worries include lack of hair, belly buttons, birth marks, spit-ups to projectile vomiting, the state of her breasts, no sleep and too much sleep!

Many mothers are almost too well read, with a vast array of baby books now available and the internet to turn to in an instant. They have often lost touch with their maternal instinct, or not given themselves a chance to connect with it. Their heads may be spinning with theories and questions about feeding, sleep patterns, and whether to use a dummy or not.

Sometimes new mothers have been discharged from the postnatal ward, where they have had good support, but when they get home they suddenly feel scared and uncertain of what to do. Step back and allow and encourage them to 'feel' what needs doing. I firmly believe and have been taught by mothers that they know their baby best! They may often be reeling from a barrage of conflicting professional advice.

> 'The evidence from history and cultures all over the world is that, by and large, women – ordinary spontaneous, loving mothers who are alert to learn from and respond to their babies – do better than all the experts put together.' Kitzinger (1992:200)

Sometimes we spend hours chatting over coffee and other times we are totally rushed off our feet. One time I caught myself holding one twin, rocking another, making soup and letting the online grocery order in!

Some doulas express concern about feeling guilty that they appear to be doing nothing and are being paid for simply sitting and listening. It is not always what we *do* but our *presence* that makes the difference.

'When I started out I remember trying to achieve everything each time I worked for the client – supporting feeding, cooking, laundry, tidying and cleaning, playing with the toddler, listening to mum etc. I then realised that I was trying to be superwoman (to show that I was good value for money) – but that that really wasn't very supportive of a new mum who is feeling vulnerable.

I now still try to be very practical and helpful around the house, but also realise that a calm, encouraging, non-judgmental, positive presence is the most important thing.'

I have felt honoured to be invited to private family occasions like naming ceremonies. Recently I had a wonderful day when I was employed to look after twins (with the au pair girl!) at a wedding combined with a baptism.

I have also been present at the sad ceremony held for a baby who did not survive.

Sadly, many of the women I support have difficult relationships with their own mothers. There are often unresolved histories and unexpressed resentment that they have somehow been failed. I have worked with families where the partners are totally relieved when I arrive so they can go back to work with no guilt, and others who think they know better than me because they have read books and want to be Gina Ford disciples! I had to gently inform one dad that he couldn't expect his newborn to sleep through the night, or indeed be in her own nursery, at one week old!

A lovely aspect of working as a postnatal doula is seeing the changes in the babies over the weeks and months spent with them. As I work predominantly with twins I am used to really tiny babies with legs that always make me think of skinny baby chicks. (Except recent twins who were astonishing at 8lb 5oz and 7lb 4oz at 38 weeks!) When I leave they are no longer helpless mites but chubby smiling babies.

As a postnatal doula you will encounter various extremes of lifestyles depending on the geographical area that you work in, from the very privileged to clients with huge practical challenges.

You will see a wide variation in personal situations. For example, some women I have worked with have gone to extreme lengths to produce a long-awaited baby. One had secretly stopped taking the pill as her partner never wanted children. Her maternal longing was so powerful that she went ahead regardless. When she was told she had conceived twins her partner went totally berserk and their already rocky relationship went from bad to worse. She knew it was her decision and although he eventually 'came round' she was initially on her own with no emotional support and that's why a postnatal doula was so essential. There were no regrets on her part and she totally embraced the joy of motherhood and her babies.

Another woman, after eight years with a partner who clearly did not want children, took the decision to have IVF regardless and conceived twins. She was delighted but scared of the loneliness and anticipated needing a lot of help, so she booked me.

Overall the nature of this work will keep you flexible and open to all lifestyles. The bonus is being continuously rewarded with the satisfaction of really making a difference. There is further comprehensive information for those considering a career as a postnatal doula in Chapter 9.

CHAPTER 2
Babies – what you need to know

Normal baby characteristics

Mothers can sometimes be shocked that their long-awaited baby is not the perfect bundle they were expecting. It can be particularly daunting if they have not had prior contact with a newborn baby, which is common nowadays.

'In delivery room scenes on TV and in the movies, the mother-to-be, often a famous actress in full makeup and with every hair in place "delivers" a baby after a few token grunts and groans. Seconds later, the doctor presents the glowing parents with a picture-perfect, neatly combed and scrubbed, cooing several-month-old infant.'

Mothers can also be unprepared for the sudden changes that can take place in their perfect, unblemished babies. If you are familiar with these you can provide reassurance and suggestions.

'I remember when she was born and turning to my husband to say "Oh my God, she's got bow legs!" and immediately thinking that she would need surgery. I

---

* See kidshealth.org/parent/pregnancy_center/childbirth/newborn_variations.html

didn't realize that this was perfectly normal. She was hairy, too, and had big red blotches on her eyes from the birth and a cone shaped head and swollen nipples.'
Smith (2009:14)

After delivery and prior to hospital discharge the baby will have a full baby check from a paediatrician. Mothers and babies in the UK will be visited at home by a community midwife (not every day) for up to ten days after the birth (more if there are ongoing issues).

It can be helpful if you are familiar with the normal behaviour, appearance and characteristics of a full-term (born after 37 weeks) newborn baby. Always refer to a professional if you are uncertain of anything.

> *Newborn stools (poo).* Immediately after delivery and for the first few days babies will pass a black, sticky tarry-looking stool called meconium. After a few days the changing poo then goes more green and then within a week will appear yellow.

> Be aware that it is quite normal for babies to do *very* loud farts, sounding almost like adults!

> *Washing newborns.* Latest guidelines recommend minimal bathing in the early weeks, with no soap or products to be used. It is beneficial to leave the vernix covering the skin as this acts as a valuable protection and will be gradually absorbed. Discourage the mother from using scented products herself as this could mask her natural smell and interfere with bonding.

> *Nappy changing.* When cleaning girls, always wipe from front to back to avoid introducing infection from the anus to the vagina. With boys, avoid pulling back the foreskin.

> *Cord care.* The area around the 'stump' should not be rubbed or cleaned vigorously. Airing is important to help the healing process and folding the top of the nappy down will help in avoiding rubbing or overheating the area.

New product

Special Delivery Instructions
Handle with care. Feed on demand.
Possible Features

- mishapen head
- cradle cap
- puffy eyes
- bent ears
- red or purple 'stork marks'
- fine hair on back + arms
- dry peeling skin
- slight swelling of male + female genitalia

- sticky eyes
- squashed nose
- white spots around nose
- quivering chin
- red rash
- blueish hands + feet
- slight swelling of breasts
- vernix in creases
- bowlegs
- mini period (in girls)

CAUTION: Bathe **ONLY** in water
use cotton wool   or   natural sponge
Baby wipes and soap not recommended for first month.

> *Cradle cap.* This is very common and can be quite unsightly, looking like a bad case of dandruff, or greasy yellow scales. Don't be tempted to pick at it or rub it away. Usually cradle cap clears up on its own, but it can be helped by gentle hair washing and massaging with almond or olive oil. If it starts to look raw or infected, suggest that the baby is seen by the GP.

> *Breathing.* Newborn babies breathe in cycles. Sometimes slow and shallow, other times getting faster and deeper. You may often notice a pause in breathing for a few seconds that soon returns to normal. If you want to check the breathing you can a) put your cheek next to the baby's mouth and nose and feel the breath against your own skin, b) look at the chest, which should be rising and falling, and c) put your ear next to the baby's nose and mouth to listen to breathing sounds.

> NEVER leave a newborn unattended on a changing table, as although they appear to be stationary they can wriggle and move and potentially fall.

> Be armed with a muslin at all times! As well as frequent dribbling, spitting up (posseting) and occasional projectile vomiting, babies can do very explosive poos, so always ensure they are protected with an old towel or nappy.

> Babies do make a surprising amount of noise when breathing… snorts, snuffles and little grunts. However, CALL THE DOCTOR IF YOU OBSERVE ANY OF THE FOLLOWING:

>> More than 60 breaths a minute.

>> Persistent grunting at the end of each breath.

>> Flared nostrils, which indicates an increased effort to breathe.

>> A high-pitched rasping sound and barking cough.

>> Retractions: when the muscles in your baby's chest (under the ribs) and neck visibly go in and out much more deeply than usual.

>> Breathing which stops for longer than 10 seconds.

>> A blue-coloured, triangular shape on and around his forehead, nose and lips meaning the blood is not receiving enough oxygen from his lungs.[*]

> Newborn babies can often alarm their parents with their quivering chins and trembling hands and startle

[*] See babycentre.co.uk/a558559/your-babys-breathing-whats-normal

(Moro) reflex. You can reassure parents that this is normal newborn baby behaviour: they are not anxious, or suffering from nerves, just experiencing normal reactions from their underdeveloped nervous systems. It normally passes after about three months. Swaddling in the early days will 'contain' this action, which will otherwise often wake a baby up (see page 38).

> *Jaundice*. This common condition is considered normal, occurring in over half of all new babies. After a few days the skin will become slightly yellow due to the presence of a chemical, bilirubin. The immature liver of a newborn is unable to process this chemical. The condition goes away on its own, usually by the end of the first week. It will only need specialist treatment if it persists and becomes severe. The midwife may advise more frequent feeding to assist the clearing of the jaundice. Babies are often more sleepy with jaundice and may need waking for feeds. You can suggest exposure to indirect sunlight, which is beneficial; place baby's cot near a window.

> Be aware that things may have changed so avoid giving outdated advice. For example, talcum powder is no longer recommended for use on young babies, as particles in talc have been found to cause lung damage and there are links to ovarian cancer. Also, newborn babies do not need extra water.

> Be familiar with the guidelines for avoiding SIDS (Sudden Infant Death Syndrome, often referred to as 'cot death'). Since these guidelines were introduced the number of deaths has fallen by over 50 per cent.

> Be familiar with current baby care advice so you can answer this sort of question:

>> When can I bath the baby? Should I use soap, nappy cream?

>> How do I know my baby is eating enough?

>> When can I introduce a bottle/dummy?

Reducing the risk of SIDS

Advice produced jointly by FSID and the Department of Health outlines the key steps parents can take to reduce the risk of cot death, including:

> Place your baby on the back to sleep, in a cot in a room with you.

> Do not smoke in pregnancy or let anyone smoke in the same room as your baby.

> Do not share a bed with your baby if you have been drinking alcohol, if you take drugs or if you are a smoker.

> Never sleep with your baby on a sofa or armchair.

> Do not let your baby get too hot and keep your baby's head uncovered.

> Place your baby in the 'feet to foot' position.

www.fsid.org.uk

>> What are the latest guidelines on storing expressed breast milk (EBM) and formula?

I recommend having an excellent reference book for yourself (for example *What to Expect in the First Year* by Heidi Murkoff), and remember to recommend that mothers ask their midwife if you are not sure about anything. When asked about how much to feed suggest they ask their midwife/health visitor, as guidelines differ for weight and gestation.

Crying

'Your baby's cry is meant to be disturbing, for it is his most important means of communication. Only by crying can he let you know that he needs you to help him – to come to his rescue.' *The Womanly Art of Breastfeeding*, La Leche League International

New mothers can be easily disheartened if they are unable to immediately calm and soothe their babies.

This can lead to feelings of frustration and being totally overwhelmed. It can take time for them to read their babies cues. 'First time parents are no more likely than experienced parents to have a baby who cries more than average in the first 3 months.' Murray and Andrews (2009).

Sheila Kitzinger has done extensive research on the subject and dispels many misleading myths and misconceptions about why babies cry (*Understanding Your Crying Baby*, 1992). She states:

> There is *no* evidence that babies cry inconsolably as a result of their mothers being stressed and tense. 'It seems that babies have their own personalities and do not merely reflect their mothers' moods.' Boys do not cry more than girls.

> Babies do not cry because they are overfed.

> Babies do not cry because they are underfed. A seriously underfed baby tends to be quiet and make whimpering sounds rather than crying vigorously.

> Babies don't cry because they have air bubbles trapped in their tummies. In fact, prolonged crying can *cause* these air bubbles due to the baby gasping.

> Babies don't cry more if their mother has smoked or drunk alcohol during her pregnancy.

> Crying is not related to the parent's educational level or IQ.

> Babies are not likely to cry more if they had a sibling that cried.

> Babies are not likely to cry more if there is a family history of allergies.

> Babies do not cry as a result of 'spoiling'.

What can you do?

Assure the parents that crying is the only way babies have to communicate. Don't jump in and try to 'save' the situation. It is the mother who is there twenty-four hours a day and she who is learning and will always know her baby best. Encourage her to read the baby's cues and recognise different cries and observe the baby's body language.

> Encourage the mother to 'read' the early subtle signs that babies make, *before* the crying develops into inconsolable crying. Newborn babies will communicate with yawns, rooting, sucking, grimaces, frowns, pulling away, looking away, arching their backs and rubbing their eyes.

> Help her to try to ascertain the cause:

>> *Hungry.* Feed me.

>> *Not hungry.* Stop 'trying' to feed me.

>> *More hungry.* Could be a growth spurt. Can occur any time, but commonly at three weeks, six weeks and three months. Increase the frequency of my feeds.

>> *Hot, cold.* Unwrap me, wrap me.

>> *Tired.* 'Help' me to sleep.

>> *Tired of being handled.* Put me down.

>> *Tummy ache/wind.* Gently massage my tummy.

>> *Got a cold/stuffy nose.* Keep upright so nose can drain.

>> *Want to be close to mummy.* Cuddle me.

>> *Don't feel well... poorly?* Check temperature, check for a rash. Take to the doctor to check for an infection.

>> *Bored.* Move me! Give me something to look at. Newborns enjoy gazing at mobiles and simple black and white books from as early as two weeks.

>> *Cries painfully during nappy change.* Could be dislocated hip. Check with doctor.

>> *Painful cry.* Check that nothing is pinching me (nappy?) or anything too tight, chafing or rubbing my sensitive skin.

>> *Soiled nappy.* Change my nappy.

>> *Sore bottom.* Air me, cream.

>> *Uncomfortable*. Make me a cosy nest. Try to replicate a womb-like environment with soft warm fabrics, or send mum and me back to bed for skin to skin.

> Suggest bathing followed by baby massage for calming before bed time. Some mothers attend baby massage courses. This is not essential, and you can encourage an intuitive approach with gentle stroking/massage using almond or olive oil.

> Help to gradually differentiate between night and day. Encourage this by showing clear signs to new babies. Encourage normal day time noise; there is no need to tiptoe around. Do what you normally do: hoover, listen to music, have the TV or radio on, chat. Suggest minimal disturbance during the night feeds. Keep lights dim and avoid stimulating the baby. Unless the outer clothes are wet or soiled and the baby is fretful, changing a wet nappy is not necessary at night, unless of course the baby has nappy rash.

> RESPOND TO ME! Engage, interact and provide stimulation. If the baby is fed and *not* tired, spend time with the baby. If you carry the baby around with you in a sling you can be 'hands free' and get on with your chores and she can be engaged and entertained in your world of activities and sound.

The brain is amazing.

'Research has now shown that a baby's brain will double its size in the first year. Babies are born with nearly all the brain cells that they need. However, connections need to be made between these cells in order to develop the skills they require to equip them to function well. The stimulation and interaction provided by the people around them will enable this to take place."

Five simple things can feed a child's growing brain: RESPOND, CUDDLE, RELAX, PLAY, TALK. These are

---

* See grandparents-association.org.uk/grandparenting/my-babys-brain.html

Respond to me

'From the moment I was born I needed you. If you hadn't made sure I was looked after I would not have survived. I couldn't do much, but everything I did, the sounds and the movements I made, were for you. I was asking you to respond to me so that I could live.

I feel very scared if I get no response from you. When you look at me with love in your eyes I feel safe. Your voice helps me to feel safe. Being close to you helps me to feel safe.

When you look at me I am interested in your face, and I look at you. This helps my eyes to work together. My brain builds connections for looking at other people and understanding them.

When you copy the expression on my face, this helps me to understand what I am feeling. Then I copy you, and this builds connections in my brain for understanding and managing my feelings.

When you move I copy your movements. This helps my brain to grow connections that make it possible for me to manage my own body, and to use my body to communicate with other people.

My brain works very slowly at first. But when you respond to me in the same way over and over again the connections you are helping to build grow strong. Then they can carry messages between the different parts of my brain much more quickly.'

www.hertsdirect.org/services/edlearn/css/mbb/
mbbinfoparent/mbbfivetothrivev2/17687269

your child's daily 'five to thrive' – the building blocks for a healthy brain. A healthy brain will help your child be happy in themselves, make friends and enjoy their family life, as well as being the best start for learning once they go to school. And every day will bring many opportunities to give your baby's brain what it needs to grow well.

> Swaddling – a feeling of pure 'wrapture'. Karp (2002:94)

When swaddling ensure that the baby is not likely to get overheated. Don't cover the baby's head, make sure the baby's legs and hips have room to move and bend, and suggest the use of thin fabric i.e. cotton, muslin.

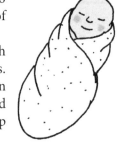

It is important to be up to date with current guidelines/recommendations. For example, recently there has been an increase in a condition called developmental dysplasia of the hip (DDH).*

> Rocking, swaying.
> Tiger in the tree. This position is easy to hold for a long time and the baby will benefit from having your warm hand on its tummy.

> Provide soothing sounds, calming music.
> Sometimes the sound of washing machines or tumble dryers calms a baby, as they provide white noise which is calming and soothing.
> Move to a darkened quiet room if the baby has got over-tired from excess stimulation.

If crying is persistent and a mother is not coping she can call Cry-sis (see Useful Contacts), which offers a helpline for parents of babies who have sleep problems or who cry excessively.

Be familiar with the digestive causes of crying: reflux, colic and wind.

One of the most common worries for new mothers and a question you will frequently be asked is: 'Do you think my baby has wind, colic or reflux?' Of course the mother's midwife is the one who should address these possible

* See **nhs.uk/news/2013/10October/Pages/Swaddling-damages-babies-hips-expert-warns.aspx**

'During the day, my main job was to try and comfort baby when she cried, and I'm a great fan of Dr Harvey Karp's five calming methods, which included swaddling baby. I'd been told by numerous doulas who had had much more experience than I had that this would help to calm all babies. Not with this one, however! She simply fought being swaddled and just got even more upset whenever I tried it! I therefore spent many hours just wandering around the opposite end of the house from Mum, bouncing and swaying baby in my arms, singing to her, making comforting shushing sounds, and trying to ensure that she was far enough away from Mum that she couldn't be heard, as the constant sound of crying was really getting Mum down. In time, baby began to relax more, and respond to more time in someone's arms, and I also encouraged Mum to have lots of skin-to-skin contact with her, which helped calm her down.'

problems. However, it is important to understand clearly the signs and symptoms. Newborn babies have to adjust from depending on an intravenous supply of food in the womb to their new independent digestive process. This adjustment can take time to work smoothly and painlessly.

Spitting up: this is a natural process where the baby can regurgitate small amounts of milk after feeds.

Wind: this is air that the baby swallows during its feeds. This air will cause them pain as it is trapped in their intestines. The only way to relieve it is if they burp or pass wind. The baby may display the wind 'characteristics' of bringing their legs up to their chest (same as colic, see below) and screwing up their face, or having a particular familiar sound to their cry.

To help relieve the wind a number of positions can be used. Encourage the mother to adopt the positions that suit her and work most effectively for the baby. There is never a need to forcefully pat the baby and no need to wind for ages, as a burp is *not* always forthcoming. Some babies are soothed by a warm bath and or massage. Try holding the baby over the shoulder, against chest, on lap, rubbing gently with upwards strokes. Lie the baby on its back and 'bicycle' the legs.

Reflux

This is when a baby experiences heartburn. An immature valve at the base of the oesophagus means that food does not 'stay down' and is brought back up with stomach acid, which causes the baby pain. The pain can be from the stomach acid hurting the throat and sometimes leads to vomiting.

Take time over feeds. Don't pat when winding or jostle about after a feed. These actions only worsen the situation.

It can be helpful to raise the cot mattress by using one or two books under the mattress, a folded towel or a specially-designed baby wedge. Once the cot is elevated to 45 degrees the baby will benefit from this propped up position.

Medication is often prescribed.

Colic

'Babies with digestive problems nearly always have colic. Research has shown that only approximately 10–15 per cent of babies are diagnosed with colic by their doctors.'
Murray and Andrews, 2009

Colic is a very common complaint in babies during the first few months. It is thought to be severe wind that causes stomach aches and griping pain. Crying most often occurs in the late afternoon or evening, with the baby drawing its knees up to its abdomen, and/or arching its back during crying bouts. The baby will have bouts of inconsolable crying and often go red in the face. Formula-fed and breastfed babies are equally affected by this condition. It has been historically described as a baby crying for more than three hours a day, for more than three days a week, for at least three weeks. However, it is more loosely described nowadays as starting in the first weeks of life and resolving by around four months of age. Despite years of research there is no known cause. Karp (2002) states that colic is just as likely to occur with a fifth baby as it is with the first. This reassures new mothers that it is not necessarily their own anxiety that is causing the baby stress.

'Infantile colic is defined for clinical purposes as repeated episodes of excessive and inconsolable crying in an infant that otherwise appears to be healthy and thriving.'*

The following helping strategies are suggested by NICE:

> Reassure parents that the colic *will* resolve in time.

> Comfort the baby by holding them during the crying episode.

> Provide gentle motion by pushing the baby in the pram or gentle rocking.

> Place them near white noise: washing machine, tumble dryer, vacuum cleaner, hairdryer or running water.

> Give them a warm bath.

There is currently no scientific evidence that confirms the benefits of the use of colic medication. Some mothers, in my experience, have found that cranial osteopathy has helped.

Crying and sleep

'Popular beliefs about when babies should be "sleeping through the night" are based on studies conducted in the 1950s and 1960s on groups of formula-fed babies. However, it is normal for babies – especially breastfed babies – to wake and feed at night throughout at least the first year.'**

'It is important to remember that babies operate according to their own internal biological rhythms and they are unaware of what their parents are being told. It often takes

---

* See patient.co.uk/health/baby-colic-leaflet
** See isisonline.org.uk/how_babies_sleep/normal_sleep_development

several months for a baby's day-night pattern of wake and sleep to become established. During this time many parents just need reassurance that their baby is normal, and that their baby's sleep patterns are developing as expected. In cases where we are unhappy with our infant's sleep development it may not be the baby that is problematic, but our expectations regarding sleep and babies' needs."

New mothers often worry that their friends' babies are already sleeping through the night, which is often not true. Every baby is unique and their age, gestation, weight, temperament and environment can all play a part in a baby's sleep pattern. I always try to encourage the mother to take time to learn her baby's cues and respond accordingly, rather than to try and 'train' them to sleep through the night when this is not appropriate for a newborn.

What can you do?

> Baby just *not* tired? New parents are often unaware of how soon a new baby is ready to be stimulated with images and objects. This little one is just two weeks old and clearly fascinated by the black and white images. He was not crying because he was tired!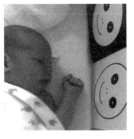

> Stop trying to get them to sleep. 'Change the subject' – move into a different space, perhaps a quieter area of the house. Share calming techniques, swaddling, using a sling, motion, rocking, bathing, and baby massage. Try a wrapped hot water bottle in the crib before putting baby in: remove the hot water bottle and always check the temperature of the sheets with your hand first.

> Suggest the use of a sling. Baby will be comforted by her mother's warmth, smell and movements. This is a

---

* See **www.isisonline.org.uk/how_babies_sleep**

'When my children were born I found it natural for me to carry them close to me. With my first son we used a baby carrier but I personally didn't always find the carrier comfortable, especially later on when he was bigger, so often it was his dad who carried him. Our son was happy in the carrier  and went to sleep easily but I think the real benefit of carrying my baby I got with my second son when using a sling.

If I had just known about slings before. A friend of mine showed me her sling. After practising a couple of times with a baby doll belonging to my friend's daughter, I found it easy to put on. The sling was very soft and stretchy which was comfortable to wear over the shoulders and I loved the warm colour too.

My second son often became unsettled and cried more often in the afternoon when I needed to pick up the older one from nursery, had to cook dinner or was outside at the playground with my toddler. As soon as I put him in the sling, carrying him around the house and outside, he felt safe and he calmed down. The sling practically moulds to the baby's body and I didn't set a foot outside without having him there as I knew he would sleep or be happy being so close to me. As the sling was a stretchy sling I could almost tuck him away which helped when it was windy for instance.'

worldwide custom that is not only practical, but has also been proven to result in more settled babies.

> Try cranial osteopathy.

Cranial osteopathy

Seeing a cranial osteopath may be a good idea if your baby is unhappy, irritable or crying for long periods, having trouble getting to or staying asleep, showing signs of digestive discomfort such as arching, drawing knees up and straining, or if you have difficulty winding, there is excessive posseting, if baby is having difficulty latching, or is only comfortable in certain positions. If you have had a caesarean section or difficult or distressing labour it might also be helpful.

Osteopaths use their highly trained palpating skills to detect areas of tension or restriction in the body, and gently release them with special techniques to restore a state of balance. It is gentle, safe and very effective for babies who usually fall asleep. No one is too young or old for treatment, and you can seek treatment as soon as you feel ready. I am yet to have a disappointed family and I have been treating babies for eight years! Babies respond very quickly to cranial treatment and usually only need a few sessions to have them feeling much better and happier.

Shellie Poulter, Osteopath, Cranial Osteopath,
Naturopath, Modern Acupuncturist

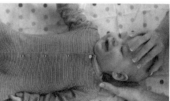

CHAPTER 3
Mothers – what you need to know

Physical

Having had babies yourself does not guarantee that you have first-hand knowledge of all or any of the things listed below. If you have not had a baby it is essential that you are aware of what is normal so that you can answer any questions clearly (for example, should I still be bleeding? Why am I peeing and sweating so much?)

Whether she has had a vaginal or caesarean birth, a new mother can experience a variety of different symptoms:

> Afterpains in the abdomen, as it contracts. Check whether she is taking regular pain relief as it is easy to forget in the blur of things, and remind her to take them on time.

> Vaginal bleeding, not unlike a period, diminishing over the following days.

> Constipation, haemorrhoids.

> Exhaustion.

> Pain in perineum following a vaginal delivery, particularly if she has had stitches.

> Pain around incision following a caesarean. This can be followed by some numbness.

> Increased sweating and urination, as the body rids itself

of the excess fluids accumulated in pregnancy or from IV fluids during labour.

> Tender, engorged breasts around three days after the birth.

A new mother may complain that her stomach is still big and that she still looks pregnant. Give reassurance that it is perfectly normal to look six months pregnant for several weeks or even months after delivery.

Following childbirth a woman will probably be sleep deprived. This will be due partly to discomfort having affected her sleep in the months prior to birth, lost sleep during a long labour and/or being awake regularly to feed during the night. Her stress levels are likely to be increased by the anxieties of the new experience, and the worry and responsibility of a new baby. Her diet may be lacking in substance due to 'forgetting' to eat or snatching 'empty calorie' snacks. All these factors can quickly contribute to her becoming run down and therefore more susceptible to infection and exhaustion. It is important to be aware of this so you can help her avoid problems. Cooking, and giving her opportunities to rest, are just two examples of how you might do this.

As you may be alone with a new mother it is important to be aware of any medical danger signs and know when to refer for medical help:

> Sudden excess bright red blood loss, large clots. Bleeding with bad odour.

> Prolonged raised temperature.

> Swelling or pain in legs.

> Severe headache.

> Vomiting not related to digestive upset.

> Dizziness.

> Pain or difficulty during urination.

> Swelling, increased redness, oozing from a caesarean section wound.

Emotional

New mothers can be on an emotional rollercoaster as they are affected by an influx of powerful hormones following birth. These hormonal changes can contribute to the upheaval of new motherhood. Mothers can experience extremes of joy and elation from the delivery of their new baby, only to be presented with the exhaustion and stress that can come from the overwhelming shock of the new responsibility of caring for a new baby and lack of sleep. Your presence can provide a safe, protective and rational atmosphere when the mother may feel agitated or out of control during this vulnerable time.

A mother may feel that the old life she knew is being wrenched away, leaving her scared and insecure about what new challenge each day will bring. If you can help create a safe and homely environment the mother, in turn, will be better placed to create those feelings for her own baby. Women can suddenly become aware of what their own mothers went through or gave them. If they are not around for them they can get upset and very emotional as they realise how, at this time, they would have appreciated them. A lot of reassurance and TLC (tender loving care!) will be needed here.

Depending on their birth experience and whether they feel comfortable with you new mothers may wish to discuss their recent birth. It can take time to assimilate and some may be in shock or highly stressed. If you feel they need professional help it may be helpful to signpost them to debriefing with a professional, such as a midwife, or recommend Birthcrisis (see Useful contacts). All worries and concerns expressed by mothers are valid. It is important to acknowledge this. She may reveal things that she does not wish to share with other family members or friends, so remember to respect confidentiality at all times.

Partners may choose to confide in you or complain about their partners. This can be quite awkward and it is clearly important to remain impartial without being judgmental.

Support but don't take sides. Your calm presence can often diffuse a situation charged with conflict.

A new baby involves a huge adjustment and a brand new lifestyle. Parents may be grieving, mourning, or missing their old life, when they could be more spontaneous, knew where they stood and had control. Early motherhood does not allow for this. It demands letting go of rigidity and being flexible to the irregular needs of babies.

Mothers can experience any or all of the following:

> Mood swings. Baby blues (see below).

> Feelings of being overwhelmed by everything! Noticeably these are things that would not have challenged them before.

> Nerves around the new responsibility of a baby.

> Frustration over all the new things to learn… feeding, dressing, bathing and settling the baby, using baby equipment and so on.

What can you do?

> Put things in perspective: 'no wonder you're exhausted!'

'Have you ever done a 24-hour-a-day job before? Where you have to wake up every two hours? Without a break? Or any days off. And did you start this job immediately after undergoing a painful, major medical procedure? Where you may have lost a lot of blood and/or been injected with strong prescription drugs. AND did this job involve a major, irreversible change in your role in life, with serious emotional ramifications (most of them good)?' Kate Evans (2009:67)

Allow the mother to feel safe and unjudged if she is in a 'mood'. Due to stress and sleep deprivation women can be snappy or distant. It is important not to take things personally.

'...we don't always have to be nice, pretty or gentle. We just have to be real, but sometimes even fierce, to protect our own space and get our needs met' Romm (2002:29)

You need to know how to recognise when things are going well or not and have the courage of your convictions, even if the appreciation or acknowledgment of your actions is not always forthcoming.

Thanks are not always forthcoming or apparent. There may be a certain degree of resentment that the mother has had to ask for help, so she may be finding it difficult to accept your presence initially. Mums are often preoccupied in a 'baby' bubble, so may seem distant and detached from interacting with you.

> Be diplomatic.
> Affirm the positive and reassure.

Praise and comment on how well she is doing and what she is achieving each day with her baby. Suddenly, for the new mother, just simply having a shower or washing her hair can seem an unattainable thing. Some new mothers get into a baby 'blur' and they may lose sight of the progress they are making. It can be very reassuring to bring things in to perspective. This can be achieved by affirming the positive things that you see as the days go by. For example:

'He's so relaxed now between feeds, the wind strategies are really working.'

'That's great that you haven't needed to express for the last 24 hours. He's obviously latching so much better.'

'You look so much more comfortable and relaxed in that new feeding position.'

Baby blues

In the old days when mothers would stay in hospital for many days after delivery postnatal wards were called 'weeping wards'. Katharina, D. (1980)

'Up to seven out of 10 mums experience the baby blues, normally about three or four days after the birth. You might feel upset, down or just feel like crying for no apparent reason. In fact, many women say they can be laughing and crying at the same time – and have no idea why!

'It isn't a mild form of postnatal depression, is completely normal and the feelings usually only last for a few days. There is no treatment, but often new mums will tell us that talking openly with family or friends has helped them during these times."

Baby blues are caused mainly by the surge and crash of hormones after the birth, lack of sleep and anxieties about the new baby, such as feeding difficulties, rashes, wind and jaundice.

What can you do?

> Reassure that this *is* normal and will usually pass by approximately ten days.

> Be there to listen and encourage the mother to express her feelings rather than bottle them up.

> Give as much help as you can to enable the mother to have time to rest.

> Provide regular meals, between-meal snacks and regular drinks. Ensure adequately balanced nutrition, as when lacking certain nutrients depression, anaemia and exhaustion can be exacerbated.

> Understand what stresses the mother most and try to alleviate it. It may be laundry, or worries over other siblings, for example.

---

* see www.babyblues.nhs.uk

Practical activities and tips

Many mothers will greet you with a list of questions. Some want a quick-fix solution. This is not our job! We can make suggestions and offer resources so she can take responsibility and decide for herself.

> 'Giving information [on the other hand], implies trust and faith in the person who is making the decision. By giving information, making suggestions, and presenting options, you are expressing confidence in the mother's ability to decide what is best for her and her family. This conveys trust which is the basis of good counseling.' *The Womanly Art of Breastfeeding*

New mothers need a lot of reassurance as they are often worried about whether their baby is 'normal' and need to know that they are doing the right thing. 'How come my baby isn't smiling, cooing, or rolling over yet, compared to other babies of the same age?' Explain that all babies are different and that they haven't read the books!

New mothers can often be a target for a barrage of conflicting baby care advice from a range of professionals, friends, family and social media.

As a helper we do not want to add to the confusion. Rather we should be there to support her decision-making.

Always step back once you have shown how to do something. In this way the mother can develop her own baby-handling skills. Don't try and jump in just to make things quicker. This is counterproductive in the long run.

> 'Tell me, I'll forget
> Show me, I'll remember
> Involve me, I'll understand.'
>   Chinese proverb

What can you do?

> Give the mother/parents the opportunity to sleep when the baby sleeps. Remind them that they are on night duty. Therefore they *must* try and sleep as much as possible in the day and try to pace themselves. Remind them that newborns generally do sleep for long periods during the day during the first weeks. Therefore when there is an opportunity, grab it.

> Suggest that the new mother does *not* get dressed for the first few days, but wears pyjamas or loose, relaxing indoor clothes. If visitors see her like this they are more likely to indulge her. If she is up and dressed they may expect her to resume her former position as a host or indeed expect her to go out before she is ready.

> Encourage mothers to try and get out daily, thus avoiding going 'stir crazy' by being housebound. Even in colder, wet weather a newborn can be well protected from the elements snuggled in the pram. The fresh air is good for the baby and can be exhilarating for the mother.

> Recommend Mumsnet if appropriate:

'We know that the best source of advice and support comes from other mums. These days, we are unlikely to live near our extended families or the friends we grew up with and when we do have our babies we are faced with starting to build a whole new set of friends. When you are feeling tired, emotional and wondering what happened to your confidence it's hard to think about how you're going to make friends. Meetups make that easier for you because you'll find other mums feeling exactly the same. So look out for meetups local to you and make some new friends'. www.mumsnet.com

> Bathing the baby: if the mother has never bathed a baby she will be very anxious to do this. Take it slowly and explain each step. I always stress submerging the baby's feet and legs gradually so they get used to it. If they are just plopped in with no warning they will cry and mothers then think

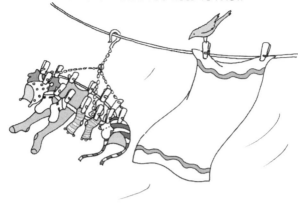

they don't like the bath, which they will eventually. Show her first, then help and then watch her do it herself.

> If hanging washing outside suggest buying at least one multi-peg hanger (inexpensive). This saves a lot of time with all the tiny fiddly clothes. It can easily be grabbed off the line in case of rain.

> Babygros. Do lower poppers up first and then 'insert' baby like putting on a pair of trousers, rather than trying to line up the poppers once baby is lying on the flat babygro. This can be really tricky, particularly in semi-darkness.

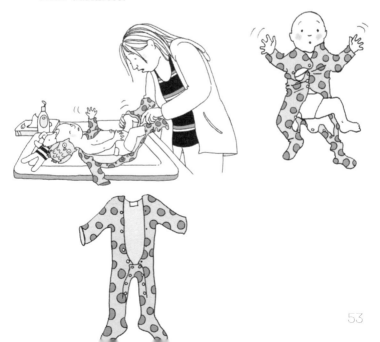

> Change the bed linen. Bed linen is soiled quicker than usual as the new mother may be 'based' in bed at first. She will be sweating more, there may be milk leaking, leaking nappies, baby sick. If she is agreeable for you to do it for her there is nothing nicer than to get back into a fresh bed after a shower or bath.

> As you will be operating/working in someone else's house it is important to put your own standards to one side. Be prepared to work in all levels of cleanliness. You may be in homes where there are literally no clean surfaces to cook on and no clean crockery or cutlery available. In contrast in some homes you will be hard pushed to actually find anything to do because the kitchens are so immaculate. Babies are generally used to whatever germs/environment they have been born into. We need to take the lead from mothers and follow and respect their standards. If they are operating a totally sanitised environment, that is what we will follow, such as cleaning the changing mat after every nappy change with antibacterial spray. If on the other hand they are happy for the family pet to lick the baby, then that too is their choice. (In a Nepalese orphanage I had to remove the ants from the baby beakers before they were used, but this was normal for them! See Appendix 3).

> Fridges. Very often new mothers are so busy with the baby that things get overlooked. Check for out-of-

date items. Often food bought before the birth needs throwing away.

> Filters for dishwashers and tumble dryers often get neglected. Do check otherwise they won't work efficiently.

> Listen out for doorbells. There are usually extra deliveries after births and it is important to avoid disturbing a resting mum.

> Suggest changing messages on phones to something like 'Thanks for all your messages, just to let you know we are fine and the baby is doing well. Will call you after our "babymoon".'

> Offer to take photos of 'firsts' – first bath, first trip out.

> Indoor plants and flowers may need regular attention.

> Fill the freezer with extra ready meals if time.

> Put shopping away.

> Be prepared to do whatever it takes for the mother to feel more in control. If this means ironing babygros… so be it! I was asked to do this once.

> Visitors. I always stress that as lovely as it is to have visitors, it can be very draining. Some just want to see the baby and hear the birth story, which mums may be tired of telling. Some are brilliant, bringing meals or providing practical help. In one twin family I worked for the father would ask what meals visitors were bringing. The parents also had a list on the fridge door which said 'Jobs for visitors: clean the surfaces, empty the dishwasher, fold the laundry…'

> Some families invite everyone to the hospital or home as soon as the baby is born. This can work well in that their families will feel happy and reassured that all is well. Some decide to ward off everyone for several days or even up to two weeks. In this way the new parents can enjoy their private 'babymoon'.

Overdoing it? I often liken the postnatal period to convalescence, from a bad bout of the flu for example, when there is a gradual improvement over time. You think you are better and then overdo it and end up back in bed. Help the mother prioritise and suggest ways she can pace herself, otherwise she will want to do everything all at once when the baby is asleep. She may feel overwhelmed by the thank you cards, birth announcements, accumulation of gifts, backlog of washing, emails to reply to, texts to reply to and so on. Remind her that the early days fly past so fast, and if she is doing too many other things she will miss precious early moments.

> Recommend activities. Babies change fast! Within weeks new babies go from sleeping a lot to being increasingly awake. They do not always want to be placed straight back in their cots. Encourage different activities from fairly early on, including time on a play mat, or under a baby gym. Tummy time is very important… encourage this from the first few weeks. Place baby on its tummy to encourage strengthening and stretching. As babies spend so much time on their backs this is important. With rocker chairs or similar start with a few minutes and gradually increase the time. Often I see a bewildered mum with a fretful baby, wondering what the matter is. She is often pleasantly surprised and relieved that the baby is well ready for a change of scene. Baby chairs can be easily carried around and placed on the floor in the bathroom while mum has a shower, or placed safely on a kitchen table so they can have eye contact and be stimulated by mum's activities. There is no need for expensive equipment. One inventive mum with twins stretched some string across the travel cot and hung up wooden spoons and coloured feathers. The babies were enthralled for ages.

> Mothers can be overly worried about every tiny thing. Reassure them that most new mothers have the same anxieties in the beginning. It is *normal*. They may come home from baby groups and panic that their baby is

not sleeping through the night, smiling or grabbing things yet. Reassure them that it is fine to be aware of the expected timings but that all babies are different and will do things in their own time.

> '...I am worried about their development though. They are not smiling yet, even though the book says they should be. Maybe they don't find life very amusing. Maybe they're Goths. Or maybe they are developmentally challenged...' Clune (2006: 218)

New mothers can get frustrated. As soon as they feel they understand the baby's needs and patterns of behaviour, they change. 'The only constant in the job of parenting is change.' Hogg (2005:3)

Encourage mothers and remind them to be flexible to their baby's changes. Make suggestions as the needs change: nappy off, kicking time, and tummy time for example.

> Mothers can get easily despondent as they are continually performing repetitive tasks. Try to emphasise all her achievements and confirm that the baby is happy and content. Sometimes it is easy for them to lose perspective and feel they are on a treadmill of thankless, invisible actions.

> Suggest mothers schedule in extra time when going to appointments. Getting out of the house can be an organisational mission! Babies are unpredictable. They may fill their nappies, get hungry or be sick just as the mother is ready to go out.

> Encourage activities, from a walk to the end of road and back to baby clubs. At the same time keep an eye on whether the mother is overexerting herself (she may complain of increased blood loss, for example). Keep the balance by ensuring she doesn't bounce back *too* quickly.

> Make suggestions from the many local options available.

> 'I never felt pressured to do anything, in fact often didn't realise that I was "doing" what had been very subtly suggested thinking it was my idea! It was only on reflection after she left that I realised what I was doing.'

For example Children's Centres, church clubs, NCT, swimming, postnatal yoga and so on. One daily activity is usually enough to enable mum to see others and baby to get stimulation. However, going to too many can exhaust everyone.

> A little while before you leave always check that mother has everything at hand that she needs – refreshments, phone etc. Check whether she has any last-minute requests before you leave.

Communication skills

It is essential that you can be a good listener. Be empathic.

> Your body language and posture should imply that you are focused and attentive. Sit forward in an open way and do not cross your arms while listening. Eye-to-eye contact is essential.

> Don't fidget or fiddle whilst listening and don't try and do anything else at the same time.

> Don't try and give immediate answers or solutions. Leave a space once you have listened to the mother.

> Put your personal opinions and history to one side.

> Feedback clearly what you understand the problem to be. This shows that you have been listening attentively.

> Make suggestions, *don't* give advice. Ways to make suggestions:

> > 'Some mothers find this helpful... Floradix tonic/ Spatone for low energy/lavender oil in the bath for relaxation.'

> > 'I have seen some good results from this, but

obviously all babies are different… Cranial osteopathy/gripe water for colic.'

> 'How do you feel about feeding lying down with the baby?'

Nutrition

It is important to be aware of what makes up a healthy balanced diet, so that you can prepare nourishing snacks and meals for the new mother.

NICE guidelines recommend a healthy diet that does *not* have to be modified whilst breastfeeding.

Myth: 'There are lots of things breastfeeding mums can't eat and drink'

Breastfeeding Mums can eat and drink pretty much anything! There are more myths about eating and drinking while breastfeeding than anything I've ever come across. A mum who is drinking enough caffeine to upset her baby might want to reduce it for her own health anyway. Yes, you can have a glass of wine. And where DID the chocolate myth come from? Or the grapes, lemons and spices?

Evolution would have played us a pretty weird trick if suddenly a human mother had to completely remove herself from the diet of her tribe. Since when have you seen cows stop eating grass because they've had a calf?

Maddie McMahon

What can you do?

> Stress the idea of good nutrition or nourishing food rather than 'diet', as this can immediately put up barriers. Nourishment and nurturing both mean 'to feed'.

'When I was upstairs feeding my baby I could smell wonderful cooking coming upstairs. It reminded me of being at home as a child with my mother downstairs creating an atmosphere of comfort and security.'

> Provide nutritious and delicious food. New mothers, whether breastfeeding or bottle-feeding, can have quite depleted reserves of energy. They are usually ravenous! We can encourage them to replenish their reserves by providing tempting food. By this I don't mean you have to be a gourmet cook. What would you prefer – a plain ham sandwich or a carefully prepared homemade stew/soup/salad? (See the recipes on pages 154–163).

> New mothers can often be constipated, so encourage plenty of fresh fruit and vegetables and plenty of water.

> They may need extra iron. Encourage plenty of dark green leafy vegetables, red meat (if the mother normally eats it), lentils and apricots.

> Encourage adequate hydration. Breastfeeding mothers usually find themselves extra thirsty whilst feeding. This can be due to an increase in oxytocin levels when a let-down reflex occurs. Ensure they always have drinks handy.

> We are there to monitor food and drink intake. By this I do not mean police it! Snacks of chocolate and biscuits are fine in moderation, but if totally depended on for energy boosts can quickly leave mothers exhausted from food containing empty calories and craving more. Remember that breastfeeding mothers will benefit from an increase of up to 500 calories a day. Provide nutrient-packed foods: dairy produce, chicken, fish, whole grains, nuts and dried fruit.

> On arrival check when the mother last ate and 'rush' her a snack if it's more than two hours.

> Often mothers are obsessed with immediate weight loss. Try and encourage them to build their health and strength through good nutrition and gradual gentle exercise, rather than crash dieting and/or obsessive exercising.

> Always ensure there is a jug and glass or bottle of water wherever the mother may be, such as next to the bed, or her favourite armchair. Encourage drinking plenty, but remember that 'over' drinking is not beneficial to milk production. Increasing water intake does not increase the milk supply. Increasing the frequency of breastfeeds will do this.

> I usually pack two plastic boxes with a nut and dried fruit mix so one can be by the bedside. Breastfeeding mothers can get hungry overnight. Because we are not used to eating at night they may ignore these signs. Assure them it is quite normal and indeed very important to eat at night to keep up their energy. Biscuits and bananas by the bedside are good standbys.

> When going out recommend they have a drink and snack in the car in case of hold-ups or needing to stop somewhere to breastfeed before returning home.

CHAPTER 4
Partners, grandparents, friends and family

Partners
How partners may feel

Entering the world of parenthood can be filled with exciting anticipation, but for some it can also bring fear of the unknown. A new baby invariably impacts on the dynamics of a couple's relationship. Nearest and dearest can become a target for exhausted mothers. It is quite usual for the mother to become irritated, snappy and quite intolerant of you (due to being exhausted), which could cause her partner to feel rejected and sometimes excluded. The partner may suddenly be sleeping apart from the mother, for practical reasons, if he needs to be up and out early for work. The partner may find himself resenting the baby taking his place in bed and thus causing him to feel the loss of cuddles, closeness and intimacy.

'When you have a child, although you are parents by definition from day one, it can take quite a while before you actually feel like parents. Becoming a family sparks off a chain reaction which can have lingering effects on the couple's relationship, which may itself take a nosedive in the months following birth. Relate counselors report that couples who come to them with long term problems frequently identify their difficulties as having started after their first child was born.' *Baby Shock*, p82

Although the mother experiences an abundance of cuddles, nuzzles and closeness with the baby, partners can sometimes feel excluded from the bonding bubble. They can feel displaced by the baby and indirectly rejected.

Kate Evans (*Food of Love*, 2009) perfectly sums this up with her observation on what partners could be feeling:

'It's tough isn't it? You meet a woman, fall in love, have a baby, and now she's in love with someone else...' *Baby Shock*

'Partners can become so focused on the birth and delivery process that they fail to go beyond the next stage... actually having the baby in their hands to care for. What happens next? Suddenly a real baby is presented to you – your child – and it can bring back all those fears you had when you first learned that you were expecting a baby. Will I cope? Can we afford a child? Is my house big enough? Will I drop him? Can I be an effective father?' Smith, J. (2008)

There may be extra stresses: money, financial pressures and being in charge – the partner may now be the sole breadwinner – and there may be increased demands on his attention from older siblings.

Partners may experience feelings of jealousy or feeling suddenly demoted. Previously he may have depended on his partner for support – for example emotional support, or support with work concerns and so on – but he now feels that she is now completely wrapped up in the baby and less available. Her priority has changed overnight, which can be a shock. He may feel frustrated at being housebound in the evenings when previously he enjoyed the freedom of spontaneity when going out. It often takes new mothers a year or more to feel comfortable leaving the baby with a trusted sitter.

> After birth a baby and mother are a "dyad" or a "unit" and, ideally, should be separated as little as possible. The early days are a wonderful opportunity for a baby to bond with mum and it is this bond that sets the scene for all future relationships.
>
> It is not unusual for a dad to become jealous of his partner's affection for her baby; this often reflects the dad's early experience of being parented. It may be challenging to play 'second-fiddle' for your woman's affections, and to appreciate that your own bonding with your baby will follow a different process. Yet by protecting this space for relaxation, bonding, and breastfeeding, you are offering profound love and support. You and your partner can also hold your partnership dear, gently allowing it to adjust to the new dynamics of your family.
>
> Sheila Kitzinger (1992:221)

It is normal for partners to experience the baby blues. Postnatal depression in fathers is also now recognised, which will allow fathers to acknowledge their feelings and seek help. They may internalise a lot whilst supporting their partner, trying to remain strong but crumbling inside. They could be grieving the loss of their wife and life that they used to know.[*]

A study of new parents (Houlston et al, 2013:8) found that:

> 62 per cent of new parents just wanted a good night's sleep, although 18 per cent wanted someone to clean up for them.

> one in 10 found that changes in their lifestyle had a negative effect on their relationship with their partner.

> almost a quarter (24 per cent) of new parents longed for some time on their own after having a baby.

---

[*] See **www.guardian.co.uk/society/2010/sep/08/postnatal-depression-fathers-men**

Rather than dwelling on the challenges of new parenthood, it is important to be prepared to look after yourself as well as your partner, and to be equipped with tips and information to improve both the support you give and the support you find from others.

Practical suggestions for partners

If you are on paternity leave and are up helping in the night then you too need to nap during the day, as well as the mother, otherwise you will be too exhausted to provide support. Sleeping when baby sleeps is a great rule of thumb, at least once a day. Make sure you get a break out of the house so you can recharge your own batteries. Meet friends for a chat so that they can support you.

Many new fathers go round in an exhausted blur. This is well documented in a light-hearted book by a father of triplets who called his book *I Sleep at Red Lights* (Stockler, 2003).

How can you help the mother?

> Shopping: check the cupboards and keep food well stocked up.

> Find out from your partner what you can do around the house that could cause her stress if not done, for example vacuuming, putting laundry away.

> Laundry: load and run washing machine, unload it and tumble dry or hang up clothes, fold dried laundry and put it away.

> Prepare handy nutritious snacks and meals... simple things are fine!

> Check the mother drinks regularly and has a drink nearby.

> Give a foot or back massage.

> Take the baby while the mother has a nap or bath, or goes for a walk.

> Provide lifts, especially after a caesarean section (the

mother may not be able to drive for six weeks - check with her insurer).

> Screen telephone calls while the mother is napping, feeding or bathing.

> Enforce boundaries with visitors or unexpected 'well-wishers'; avoid tiring mother and baby.

> Ask friends and family in to help with some cooking or household chores. One client I had actually had a list on the fridge which said 'Jobs for visitors' and included washing up, loading the dishwasher and so on.

> If friends are coming to visit, ask them to bring a meal.

> If you are going to be coming home later than expected *do* let her know. Your imminent arrival will often be what she is holding out for, if she is having a stressful time. Realising this and pre-warning her can avoid an emotional confrontation later.

How can you help the baby?

> Nappy changing.

> Activity time… babies respond early to stimulation. Show them objects, make sounds for them to hear and try simple black and white baby books.

> Take the baby out for fresh air in the pram, or in a sling.

> Carry/soothe baby in a sling, indoors or out.

> Have skin-to-skin time.

> Bath the baby, or bath *with* the baby.

> Baby massage.

> Swaddling and settling to sleep. Encourage the mother to hand baby to you when baby is settled after a feed and preferably not when screaming inconsolably and clearly only

wanting the breast/mother. A partner can very quickly feel negative towards the new baby if it is never calm in their arms.

Grandparents, friends and family

Are you planning to help in the days following birth? If so consider the following points:

> Preferably, before the baby arrives give the mother your availability. Be clear with her what you can offer and respond to her anticipated needs. She may want you to move in for a while, pop in on specific days or be available to be called in an 'emergency'.

> Be realistic with your offer of help. She needs to know that she can rely on your commitment to her. If you know you have other commitments, such as a family birthday, or work, tell her those dates in advance.

> Do not go if you are unwell. It is better to cancel than introduce germs to a new mother and baby

Practical and personal considerations

> Always wash your hands immediately on arrival before you handle a newborn, and wash them after nappy changing. A hand sanitiser in your pocket can be useful so you can apply whenever necessary, particularly if in a hurry.

> Avoid wearing overpowering scent. A new mum doesn't want her baby handed back to her smelling of you.

> Tying back long hair is also a good idea.

> Keep nails from catching on delicate baby skin.

> Avoid protruding rings, bracelets, watches or necklaces as they can easily catch or harm babies' skin.

> Avoid wearing itchy or scratchy fabrics or fabrics that could shed or moult on the baby such as mohair.

> Gifts: however nice you may think 'smelly' gifts are, like candles, lotions and creams, remember that smell is a

very personal thing and new mothers are particularly sensitive to it. In the early days when she is bonding with her baby always give scent-free products, or better still a voucher so she can choose her own products later.

> It will be very reassuring for the new family, and indeed for you, if you have attended a paediatric first aid course so you will be confident in a medical emergency.

Grandparents

If your daughter or son has accepted your help once the baby arrives, whether it is for the odd day or you are moving in for a while, you will, I imagine, be feeling very excited and maybe a bit daunted.

It is important to be aware that since you had your children many things have changed about parenting.

'Rigid, strict routines like letting baby "cry-it-out" have been proven to be detrimental – especially to young babies. Strict feeding routines have also been proven to be harmful to both the baby's growth and the mother's breast milk production'.*

As your children become parents the family dynamic changes automatically, leading you straight into your new

---

* See McKay www.bellybelly.com.au/grandparents/how-grandparents-can-help-with-a-newborn

'I also feel that I was able to help educate the grandparents a little, and help them understand just how much support their daughter needed. It seemed that Mum had brothers and sisters who all had large families and that their children were relatively easy and therefore both Nanny and Grandad felt that my client was making rather a song and dance about bringing up her second child. I don't think they appreciated that this little granddaughter was not just being demanding, but was genuinely in pain a lot of the time, which was why she was crying. As time went by, they began to appreciate how hard it was for their daughter, and the level of support they offered her increased.'

role as grandparents. Just as parents take time to adjust to their new role, so will you. As a parent you may have always wanted to be the 'solver' and provider of answers. However, if we continue like this we will in fact disenable and disempower our children to develop their own parenting skills. This is the time to give your support and suggestions but *not* advice. It may feel difficult for you to not be in charge or to have the last word, so give yourself time to acknowledge your change of role and take a step back.

How can you help?

Do not overstep your boundaries by 'rushing in' too quickly to help. The new parents may plan to co-sleep, use slings, use a dummy (or not), feed on demand, take baby out in the first week… all things you never did. Be open and non-judgmental about their ways. Honour and respect their wishes and decisions.

> Offer practical suggestions (see previous chapter).
> Be cautious of overdoing it: although you want to be helpful, you need to avoid any suggestion that the new

parents are not capable and you need to ensure that you are not denying them or delaying the chance for them to learn and get experience of their own.

> You will need to avoid making comments that could affect their newly developing confidence and parenting skills.

> Overstepping the mark with advice will be counterproductive and could cause the new mother to become over-possessive and not wish to 'hand the baby over'.

> Although your intentions may be generous, it is usually best to ask first what you can buy for the new baby. I have often seen new mothers despairing that despite their parents' generosity they have been showered with items that they don't like or need and would have preferred to choose themselves.

> When the time is appropriate offer to babysit, even just for an hour during the day or an evening, to give the new parents some time alone together.

> Respect the other grandparents, especially over different cultural traditions. Try to balance the visits. New parents do not want to feel there is any competitiveness between grandparents.

Friends

> Even if the new mother is a close friend you may not have seen her as she is when in the grip of postnatal hormones and exhaustion. Your familiar friendship may be temporarily re-formed into a new dynamic. The new mother may become totally focused on her baby and

not want to 'chit chat' about non-baby things. You will need to be flexible and non-judgmental. She may have always been physically uninhibited with you, but could suddenly become shy and embarrassed or vice versa. So be sensitive, and respect her feelings.

> You could get together with other friends and provide a rota of help.

> If you have children it is not helpful to have them with you when visiting in the early days (especially if they may be carrying germs!), unless you know from experience that they will help/distract/entertain her children. She will need your undivided attention. If you can leave your children with someone for a few hours this will be more useful than arriving with your family in tow and hardly being able to help her.

> Avoid making negative statements like 'Poor little thing, looks like she's starving', or 'My first baby slept through the night from two weeks.' Every baby is different.

CHAPTER 5
Supporting families with older siblings, single mothers, and families with pets

Families who already have children

Often new mothers are overwhelmed with feelings of guilt that they can't give older siblings the attention they used to and can't always attend quickly enough to the new baby.

Siblings can often become very challenging with the arrival of a new baby. Biting, tantrums, aggression, eating problems, sleep disruption, toilet regression or in fact any regressive behaviour, such as renewed or increased thumb-sucking or dummy use, are all normal reactions from a child who is anxious about their place in the family. A lot of reassurance is needed here. New mothers can often be heard to say that their 'perfect' child has turned

into a monster overnight! Reassure them that this is normal and things will improve.

Be aware that even though this may be the second baby, feeding styles and sleep patterns can be noticeably different. Second babies can be more fractious due to being jogged around due to rushed feeds causing increased wind. They can get overtired as they are frequently being picked up and taken out, due to the older child's activities. On the positive side many second or third babies can be more easy-going as they just have to fit in and go with the flow!

Although the following was written about premature babies, it can be applied to all newborns:

'When the siblings want to hold or play with the baby, parents may try to discourage them for the fear that the new baby is too fragile. Picture for a moment that your toddler is thinking: "Here is a new baby that Mom is keeping to herself all the time." If you always say "no" or "be careful" or "don't touch the baby" your toddler will definitely grow to resent the new sib. She wants to interact with that baby, and if she can't do it with your help, she'll find her own angry ways of making contact.'
Sears (2004:146)

The author goes on to say:

'Allow your toddler to interact in a way that is safe. Let her kiss baby, hug baby, rub baby's tummy, pat baby's back, and play with the baby's hands and feet. Instead of saying no, show her how to love baby safely and gently. Teach her ways to play that that will not over stimulate baby.'

Do not 'force' the older sibling to interact with the new baby. They need to be allowed to show interest in their own time. Remember newborns who are doing very little can be quite boring to a toddler!

When there is more than one child it is most likely that you will be involved in more childcare activities. It is important for the mother to continue to do what she

can reasonably manage, like reading a story whilst she is feeding.

Often well-meaning helpers will try to 'take away' the older sibling(s). Although this can give the mother much-needed time alone to rest or be with the baby, it is in fact *not* always what the sibling needs. The older child needs quality time with her mother (parents) without the new baby, even if it's just for a short time. So, when possible 'remove' the *baby* into another room and look after the baby rather than the toddler. This will help to avoid the situation that

often occurs where the siblings are swept off by everyone trying to help and are over-stimulated with lots of extra activities, when in fact children thrive on the normality of their routine, and will quickly become overtired and more demanding of their parents. So a balance of distractions and normality will hopefully keep things on an even keel.

If you are helping out you will need to be good at diffusing fractious situations with imagination and distraction strategies.

What can you do to help?

Before you start, do ensure that you are clear on ground/ house rules: what food/snacks are the children allowed and when, how much TV are they allowed to watch, where is it safe to play outside, and what are the rules about where to eat? Many endearing children have tried to convince me that yes, they can have treats at any time and watch TV whenever they like!

If you are to be left in charge, for example at a meal time, whilst the mother is feeding the baby in the other room, check with the parents if they are happy for you to take charge if they are being 'naughty' or if they would rather

you called them to sort it out. Remember that you can't expect children to trust you if they don't know you.

Providing distractions
> Take the child outside, if there is a garden. Or, if the mother is happy just have a little walk outside. The children will benefit from a good blast of fresh air which will revive and calm them down if they are getting fractious.
> Cooking. Simple pastry jam-tart making (frozen pastry is easy for this), or get them involved with smoothie making. Children love to pass you things and chop simple things (age-appropriate, or just break up the fruit) like bananas.
> Washing up. If a child is capable, put a chair by the sink and fill with bubbly water and a few pots… they will be happy splashing about with a washing up brush and a few containers. Be armed with waterproofs!
> Hide and seek
> Creative activities… sticking, gluing and so on.
> Make tents using sheets or towels draped over chairs and provide a little picnic. Children seem to love their

own new 'nest' – their baby has one, so why not them?

> Suggest that mum has a stash of surprise gifts. They do not have to be expensive, just little somethings wrapped up for use in an emergency! Books, small toys and snack treats are all good ideas.

> Music. Let children dance out their energy! Or musical statues or bumps is always fun.

> Suggest the child takes a photo of their new sibling to school to share. This will make them feel special at a time they may feel the baby is getting all the attention.

> Reminding a toddler that they were a baby once can be reassuring as they can see how loved and cherished they were by seeing old photos, if available and appropriate.

> Suggest the mother has a 'special' or 'snuggle' time with the toddler *before* she needs to feed the baby, as often children are told 'When I have fed the baby I will be with you', which can make them feel they are always in second place.

Supporting single parents

You may have a friend or relation who is single and expecting a baby. They may have planned to have a baby 'alone', have split with their partner as a result of a relationship breakdown, or be alone following a bereavement. Whatever their situation they may well be facing emotional, practical and/or financial problems. The implications of this increase in stress will clearly create extra anxiety over their ability to cope once the baby arrives. Just like any new parents they will need plenty of practical and emotional support. However, the nature of your support may differ in the need for increased hours of help. Ideally your help should be well organised prior to the arrival of the baby.

How can you help?

> Where there are financial restraints help source equipment. Suggest Freecycle, Gumtree, Netmums.

> Stress that it is not necessary to have mountains of equipment. List the basics and suggest borrowing things that are only needed initially for a short time, such as a Moses basket and baby bath.

> If they have older siblings suggest they create a pick-up and drop-off for school rota. Perhaps suggest having the friend's child to play at drop-off, if appropriate, as that way the mother will feel she is reciprocating the favour.

> Suggest working out a support rota amongst the mother's friends, particularly in the early days. It will most likely be harder to get night help, but if someone can come in during the day the new mother will at least be able to have a break or sleep to 'top up' her energy levels to face the night ahead.

Suggestions

> Apply for a Homestart helper (Homestart provides a non-medical, but trained volunteer who can be provided for half a day a week for any family with a child under five.* This should be organised prior to the birth as there are waiting lists.

> Attend the local Children's Centre. These centres are open to all parents, whatever their situation, carers and children. Many of the services are free. They offer a wide range of daily activities and educational and information sessions. They will give help and advice on child and family health, parenting issues, money, training and employment.

> Single parent support groups include: Gingerbread, Netmums, Onlymums.org, Lone-parents.org.uk

Supporting a family with pets

It is estimated that at present 48 per cent of UK households have at least one pet. This is equivalent to 13 million households.** Dogs and cats are the most popular. It is clear

---

* See www.home-start.org.uk
** See www.pfma.org.uk/pet-population-2008-2012

from this statistic that many parents with new babies will also have animals.

If the pet came first it is often seen as and treated like a first child. Jealousy is the obvious reaction and may manifest in various unpredictable ways. This is very similar to a toddler reacting to a new sibling.

Many parents are not worried about their pets posing any danger to their offspring, but personally I never leave a pet alone with a newborn when I am in a position of responsibility. There have been tragic cases of well-loved and trusted family dogs 'turning' on a baby. A sudden new or startling sound could cause a predatory reaction. Even though you may be reassured that the cat can sleep in the cot with the baby, I could not relax with this happening!

Many parents are perfectly happy for their pets to lick the baby, so respect their choice in a non-judgmental way.

How can you help?

> Suggest getting a baby doll (anatomically correct size). If this is introduced a few months prior to the birth it will hopefully become familiar to the pet. But *don't* give it to the dog as a toy! A crying doll would be best, but playing baby crying noises as well would be effective preparation for the arrival of a new baby in the house.

> Allow the dog to smell a worn babygro or used sheet or muslin so that it can get used to the baby's smell.

> Suggest that when the mother and new baby return from hospital they greet the dog without the baby. If possible have the baby in another room to avoid the excited dog leaping up to greet the mother.

> Suggest the owners spend some 'quality' time each day with the pet. (Ten minutes is plenty!)
> Look after the baby while the owner takes the dog for a walk.
> Offer to walk the dog if it is missing out on regular walks.
> Suggest using a stairgate to separate the baby from the pet.
> Use a cat net on prams/buggies in the garden.

'E and L were due their first baby and had two dogs – a busy terrier and a much more laid-back dachshund. They were very much Mum's dogs – she adored them and spent a lot of time with them, whereas Dad tolerated them. She had grown up with dogs, he hadn't. She was concerned, before the baby arrived, at how the dogs would cope with the new baby in the house. We discussed different arrangements and options. When the proud parents brought their precious new baby home Mum was immediately concerned about the dogs. They were of course interested in the baby and quite excited to see their Mum, who decided the best thing to do was to take them for a short walk round the block, to give them some undivided attention and walk off some of the pent-up excitement. When Mum and dogs returned there was much discussion about how the dogs should behave around the baby – what was and wasn't appropriate. The dachshund took herself to her bed and was quite calm. However, the terrier was quite needy, wouldn't stay on his bed and kept creeping towards Mum and wanting to investigate the baby in her arms. We gave him praise and attention, but encouraged him to return to his bed. Dad got more and more anxious about the dog's behaviour, becoming quite fierce with the dog. Eventually, an hour or so later they made the decision that it would be better for the dogs to go to E's mother for a while, until E and L felt settled at home with the baby. Sadly, baby C got quite unwell and they had to spend a fair amount of time in hospital, so the dogs haven't returned home yet. I don't know if they will. I expect L would prefer it if they didn't.'

CHAPTER 6
Feeding Babies

When you support a new mother it is essential that you respect her feeding choice in a non-judgmental way, whatever method she favours. It is important that a mother feels at ease with her choice. Explain that you want what's best for her and her baby and have no investment in her choice either way.

Breastfeeding

This chapter is *not* about the mechanics of breastfeeding, or the advantages, which are well documented in the wealth of books on breastfeeding available. It is about finding ways of improving your provision of care and support on a practical and emotional level.

> 'You'll no doubt have pressure from both sides of the feeding fence! As a breastfeeding supporter who also has paid work to do and a family to look after, I don't really have time to go round pinning pregnant women against the wall and 'pressuring' them to breastfeed. There is a distinct difference between public health information and 'pressure'. I don't feel pressure not

to eat too many cream cakes. I am aware of the risks of obesity and a high-fat diet. I feel a bit guilty when I have one too many biscuits, but no one is making me feel guilty or pressuring me to eat salad. There is pressure to formula feed though – from friends and relatives who know nothing else, from TV that never shows a breastfeeding mum – or if they do, she's having problems – adverts, social networking and free gifts and 'carelines' from formula companies and mothers who have never had the chance to fully debrief from their own experiences and therefore pass their negative feelings on to other mothers. Then there are the people who liken public breastfeeding to public defecation, and who call breastfeeding women and their advocates spiteful names.

It's not as if formula is poison! There is a social taboo around talking about the risks of formula. It seems we only have permission to talk about the benefits of breastfeeding – and only if we don't 'ram our dripping breasts down people's throats'. Like every other subject that stirs passionate feelings, there are some evangelical zealots; women who are enthusiastic about breastfeeding and want to share their own happiness with others. They may know quite a bit about the risks of formula and what the baby misses out on when denied the nursing relationship. However, they may not have much experience working with mothers and therefore lack insight into the varied and complex reasons why some mothers may feed their babies formula. They don't have full knowledge of the social and commercial pressures that impede breastfeeding. They have not learnt to reserve judgment or how to use language that doesn't appear judgmental – a skill that is really difficult when everyone reacts to things in different ways.'

Maddie McMahon, Doula, Breastfeeding Counsellor & Tutor

The 2010 infant feeding survey states that after one week less than half of the women who started breastfeeding are still exclusively breastfeeding. Your presence supporting the new mother can provide her with the continuity of care she needs. You will be in a prime position to observe, encourage and most of all support her as she works through any challenges she may encounter.

Even if you breastfed your own children there are a huge range of physical and emotional feelings that you may not have experienced. Supporting a woman in the breastfeeding process is very different from actually doing it yourself. It is therefore important that you have patience and an understanding of the process. Many women sail through, but sadly many don't.

You may have unresolved issues about your own feeding experience, or indeed many unanswered questions over feeding dilemmas you may have had. If this is the case take some time to explore these issues (with help from a professional if necessary) and try to unravel any negativity you may still be holding on to. These feelings can cloud your belief in the process working and need to be removed so as to avoid any blocks that may impact on the quality of your support.

Some examples of breastfeeding difficulties I have encountered:

'I dreaded every feed due to the pain that I anticipated each time'. In this case the help of an experienced breastfeeding supporter could have resolved the positioning, which was causing the pain issue.

'He seemed to feed constantly in the first week or so and I got so sore and exhausted I gave up'. In this case if it had been explained that newborns *need* to feed a lot in the early days to stimulate milk supply and that they have such a tiny tummy capacity in the early days, the mother may have continued, especially if she had received some help to make the latch more comfortable. It would also have helped her to know that newborns may feed between twelve and twenty times in a 24-hour period.

Myth: 'Lots of women can't breastfeed. My sister's nipples nearly fell off!'

I listen to sad stories every day. It is hellish to go through such pain and disappointment. I often wonder if a properly qualified and experienced Lactation Consultant or Breastfeeding Counsellor might have been able to shed some light on their problems. When things veer away from normal and into the category of the more unusual problem, women need a properly qualified specialist – as with anything else. (I wouldn't expect a midwife to be able to perform a C-section, or a GP to be a consultant dermatologist, for example).

Maddie McMahon

'I never could tell if my baby had had enough milk'. If it had been explained that the important indications that baby is feeding satisfactorily are: baby is latching and feeding well, waking up regularly for feeds and is peeing and pooing regularly, the mother would probably have been reassured.

Lack of support and encouragement is the typical and recurring reason reported by women for giving up: *'I tried but it didn't work because I didn't get enough support'* reported 49 per cent of 2,002 Mumsnet survey respondents. (Mumsnet survey, 2009)

I have been fortunate to have successfully breastfed three babies. However, I do remember the excruciating pain of engorgement when my milk 'came in', and the barrage of conflicting advice I was given about correct positioning! It was only when I worked as a midwife on the postnatal ward that I saw for the first time the wide variety of physical problems and emotional issues that women are faced with. I remember spending many hours encouraging and providing support for distraught, exhausted women.

It is important to be sensitive and respect the woman's

feelings concerning her breasts. Some may feel uncomfortable and self-conscious. Others will 'let it all hang out'.

'The real reason I'm not breastfeeding is deeply personal and deeply embarrassing: I'm not comfortable with the concept of busting out a boob anywhere. Sometimes not even my own bedroom. Yes, I have issues. I'm well aware, as is my long-suffering husband.'

'A lot of it has to do with my being. You could say I grew up ashamed of my sexuality.'

Many women are not prepared for the realities of breastfeeding. They may have an idealised image of breastfeeding in their minds:

> 'When she first felt her son's groping mouth attach itself to her breast, a wave of sweet vibration thrilled deep inside and radiated to all parts of her body; it was similar to love, but it went beyond a lover's caress, it brought a great calm happiness, a great happy calm.' Milan Kundera

> 'I never expected breastfeeding to be so difficult and painful, and unlike giving birth there is no set period of time when the pain will be over. There didn't seem to be a light at the end of the tunnel. Thank goodness, three months into it we seemed to click, and after that it became the natural and beautiful experience I'd always envisioned.' Giles (2003:14)

Before you start supporting a new breastfeeding mother:

> Ensure that you understand the basic mechanics of breast feeding. Invest in a good book or watch online videos of

---

Three simple rules of breastfeeding

1. Feed the Baby!
2. Protect your milk supply.
3. Keep Mum and Baby together.

Maddie McMahon

> 'I take great delight in talking about the effects of oxytocin and dopamine on the pleasure centres in a mother's brain. That the sense of connection, abiding sense and calm and sometimes a superhuman burst of creative thinking, or of seeing all the colours of the world super-charged is how mother nature rewards us for nursing.'
>
> Maddie McMahon

correct positioning. Know how a good latch should look and be familiar with the feeding 'movements'. Check breast/mouth alignment and suck, pause, swallow pattern. I would highly recommend Dr Jack Newman.[*]

> Always remember the power of praise and applauding/ acknowledging the wonderful life-affirming task that the mother is doing by breastfeeding.

> Explain that as well as feeding her baby there are endless other possible experiences to be had from breastfeeding her baby.

> Comfort and preparation are crucial for both mother and baby before starting a breastfeed. Ensure that she is 'set up' and 'good to go'.

> Check that the mother has eaten within the last two hours and is well hydrated and has a drink that she can reach. The hormone oxytocin, produced during breastfeeding, can increase thirst.

> It is not necessary to over-drink, as this could have a detrimental effect on milk production. Encourage the mother to listen to her body and eat when hungry and drink when thirsty.

> Have plenty of pillows, if possible/available (otherwise improvise with rolled up towels) so that you can assist in placing them so that her back, neck and arms are

---

* See www.breastfeedinginc.ca/content.php?pagename=videos

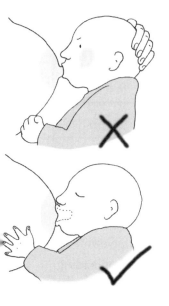

supported. Encourage her to have her feet up if possible. Be aware that there are many ways to sit when breastfeeding, and you do not always have to sit up straight. Good posture is vital so that mum is comfortable and therefore able to sustain her position, with a supported back and no strain on her neck, shoulders or arms. Leaning back a little or even reclining allows most mothers to feel very comfortable and relaxed, and gravity helps keep the baby in place on her torso, rather than her having to bear all the weight of the baby in her arms. This is known as biological nurturing and is different from the more prescriptive 'nose to nipple' advice. It is a mother-centred approach where the mother is encouraged to be inventive within the 360 degrees of attachment positions.

> Observe the latch but try not to invade the mother's space. Obviously this is a very intimate situation where you need to be sensitive to the mother. If she is very shy or self-conscious, keep your distance. Ask before you sit on the bed. Rather than stare while she is feeding find something to do, such as folding laundry, at a distance where you can observe and listen discreetly.

> Is baby comfortable and relaxed, mother not holding head or forcing/ramming? Suggest lying in bed to feed so they can both be more relaxed and will get more rest.

> Does the mother bring the baby to her breast, not stretch breast towards baby or lean forward towards the baby as if 'bottle-feeding with her breast'?

> If the baby is not 'self-attaching' in the biological nurturing position, is she bringing the baby to the breast *chin first,* so that the baby scoops up a big mouthful of

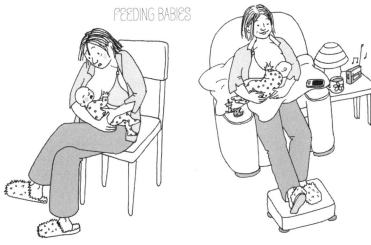

breast, with the bottom lip resting far away from the nipple, whilst the top lip skims just over the nipple? This will ensure a comfortable latch.

> Is she experiencing pain? If so, ascertain what kind. Is it the new sensitive feeling or actual shooting, jarring pain which might indicate a poor latch?

> Is she tense and anxious? If so, suggest she stops, relaxes and tries again. Explain how to release the latch by inserting a fingertip in the corner of the baby's mouth to release the suction.

> Is the nipple squished or does it look like a new lipstick when the baby comes off? If so, it's likely the latch is not quite deep enough.

Explain, when/if appropriate:

> Expressing breast milk. Not recommended during the first six weeks while breastfeeding is becoming established, except of course in emergency cases, for example prematurity.

> Babies have tiny tummies and therefore they sometimes need to feed little and often, or they may go through a growth spurt where they seem to need more feeds. These 'frequency days' are due to 'developmental leaps' and often mothers will notice that their babies are suddenly doing new, clever things – smiling, cooing, rolling over

and so on. Fortunately, once the cluster-feeding period is over, most babies will sleep deeply for several hours. Encourage mum to settle down in a feeding nest, if possible and just go with it.

> The benefits of night feeds, particularly in the early days, in order to increase/encourage milk production. Prolactin levels are higher at night, thus giving a valuable boost to the production of milk.

> How to help promote the increase of milk: increase regularity and length of feeding, encourage the mother to try slowing down if possible and increase rest, ensure regular nutritious food intake and ensure well hydrated.

> Know the content of breast milk and how it contains the perfect balance of nutrients which adjust for each stage of feeding the growing baby. Colostrum contains everything a baby needs for the first few days; hindmilk and foremilk ensure baby's feeds are well balanced; breast milk contains 90 per cent water and no extra water is needed.

> Be aware of and familiar with the symptoms of wind, colic, reflux (see Chapter 2).

> Know the latest guidelines for storing expressed breast milk: check with NICE or NHS.

> Be aware of tongue tie, a condition in which the membrane tethering the baby's tongue to his mouth is too thick and strong for the baby's tongue to move freely. This can cause pain and difficulty while breastfeeding. Tongue ties can be easily snipped by a professional for an immediate improvement in breastfeeding (see Useful Contacts).

Know when/where to signpost for extra help:

Have a good, up-to-date resource list of local support, as well as the numbers for the national breastfeeding helplines (see Useful Contacts).

Helpful tips:

> Always encourage as much physical closeness as possible between the mother and baby in the early days. This close proximity will stimulate the hormones that encourage the breastfeeding process to become established through her touching, smelling and stroking her baby.

> Discourage expressing milk or introducing bottles or dummies for the first six weeks. It takes at least this long for breastfeeding to become established.

> Sore nipples: expressed breast milk can be gently applied and then left to air dry. If the nipples are particularly damaged or dry a lanolin-based cream can be applied.

> If the mother has an abundant milk supply, suggest donating to a breastmilk bank, if appropriate. There are milk banks across the country that supply donor breastmilk to sick and premature babies. Mothers express their milk into bottles to store in the freezer, which are then collected by motorcycle courier and taken to the milk bank, where the milk is pasteurised and stored until needed. For more information see www.ukamb.org.

Formula feeding
Emotional issues

'Perhaps the biggest downside of the Breast is Best campaign is the way it can affect the emotions of mothers who formula-feed' Smith, H. (2009)

Many women are clear from the outset that they will be bottle-feeding their babies. For these there will be far fewer or no problems of conflict, guilt or anxiety over their decision/choice.

However, many are faced with a difficult decision, if breastfeeding doesn't work out and they are forced to switch from breast to bottle. This is often due to poor

support and lack of encouragement. Feelings of guilt can then ensue, followed by the feeling that they have failed themselves and their babies. Of, course there are situations where the decision is unavoidable due to maternal illness, or needing to take specific medication for postnatal depression.

Helpers need to be sensitive in this situation and do whatever it takes to support a mum through the transition.

Practical help

If you are not familiar with bottle feeding guidelines or have any queries, remember to mention the sources of support mothers can access (peer supporters, health visitor, if there are any concerns).

The evidence shows many mothers do not follow the current guidelines so it is important to be very clear, especially as partners or grandparents may have previously done it in other ways. Babies under one should have infant (first stage) formula. Follow-on and toddler milks are not suitable for babies under six months and are unnecessary

> 'If it weren't for formula, my baby would have starved! All mothers should be free to make a choice'. It must indeed be a relief to finally find the resolution to your pain – if no one is offering a solution that enables us to continue to breastfeed whilst staying sane, most mothers would agree that this doesn't leave us with much choice! Freedom of choice is of course very important indeed, so I wonder why more women aren't angrier about the lack of skilled support available to them. Lack of information and skilled support effectively takes away our free will to decide how to feed our babies.'

products; babies can stay on infant formula until they are a year old and can then consume cow's milk.

> Best practice for when out and about: use a vacuum flask for hot water, and take powder in a pre-measured pot, rather than a pre-mixed bottle in a warmer.

> If affordable it is handy to have a few ready-to-feed cartons, which you can use at room temperature, especially in the early days or when out of the house.

> Be familiar with how to assemble a breast pump and how to use a steriliser.

> Encourage the same amount of closeness as when breastfeeding by encouraging the mother or the person feeding the baby to look into baby's eyes, talking and smiling at him during feeding. Encourage skin-to-skin contact. Encourage mum to do as many of the baby's feeds herself as she can.

> Hold the baby upright so that she can breathe and swallow easily. The baby's head should be slightly higher than her body while she is feeding.

> Swap sides for feeding: this is good for both the mother's back and the baby's neck and vision.

> Night feeds: for easy and quick preparation prepare boiled water at the right temperature in a vacuum flask. Keep this along with sterilised bottles and pre-measured

Making up infant formula

Make up one feed at a time. Boil water and leave to cool for around half an hour to no less than 70 degrees C (this is hot enough to kill the bugs in the powder, but not so hot that it will denature all the ingredients). Add the powder to the water, not the other way round. Formula powder is not sterile so good hygiene is essential (many parents don't know this).

For more information see: **www.nhs.uk/conditions/ pregnancy-and-baby/pages/making-up-infant-formula.aspx**

powdered formula in the bedroom.

> Remind parents that they will need to change the size of the teat as the baby feeds more efficiently. Usually this happens after two to three months. Watch for signs that the nipple hole is too large or too small. If baby almost chokes during a feeding, milk flow may be too fast. Turn the full bottle upside-down without shaking. If milk flows instead of drips, the nipple hole is too large. If baby seems to be working hard, and tires easily during sucking, the nipple hole may be too small.

> Encouraging the parents to eat a good diet and rest when they can is important, even if they are not breastfeeding. This will ensure good health and postnatal recovery.

CHAPTER 7

Supporting families with twins or triplets, and premature babies

Twins

Many people will say to new twin parents. 'How on earth do you cope? I find it hard with just one.' A client recently told me her reply, in a matter-of-fact way: *'I have nothing to compare it to; therefore I just get on with it.'*

Useful facts

In the UK:

> About one in eighty births resulting from natural conception is a multiple.

> One in four births after IVF result in either twins or triplets.

> Twins account for about 1.5 per cent of all pregnancies.

> Perinatal mortality is five times higher in twins than singletons. The incidence of SIDS is also higher. This awareness is critical because as a doula you could be faced with unexpected grief and your support will be vital.

> Over half of twins are born by caesarean section. The reasons given to parents are: babies' position, previous caesarean, difficult vaginal delivery or previous history of placenta praevia. All monoamniotic twins are

recommended to be delivered by caesarean, although parents are of course entitled to make their own choice.

> A recent Canadian research study has been published announcing that vaginal birth is safer than C-section for twins when the first is head down. Edmonds, S. (2013)[*]

> There is a 98 per cent survival rate for babies born weighing between 2½lb/1kg and 5½lb/2.5kg.

Tips and information for supporting twin families

> Identical twins? Use a dab of nail varnish on one baby's nail.

> When you visit prior to starting to support a twin family, check equipment. If babies are predicted to be very tiny micro nappies will be the only ones that fit. Also having some tiny premature babygros is a good idea. Multipacks of vests and plenty of sheets, muslins and similar will be needed, as the volume of laundry is shocking! If possible changing areas upstairs and downstairs will save carrying everything up and down.

> Suggest the mother has plenty of nutritious snacks, such as bananas, and nuts and seeds, and a freezer full of pre-cooked meals if possible. Time will be limited for preparing food.

> Due to the increased risk of prematurity advise having a hospital bag ready from week 26.

> As one twin will go to a special care baby unit (SCBU) in 40 per cent of cases (TAMBA, see Useful Contacts) it is very helpful to have the opportunity to see the unit prior to delivery, if possible.

> Everything that can be done to discourage premature delivery will be suggested. For example: bed rest, administration of medication to halt premature labour (when appropriate). 'A day in the womb is worth a week in an incubator,' Clunes (2006:206)

---

[*] See www.news.utoronto.ca/cesarean-no-safer-vaginal-delivery-twins

> Encourage the mother to contact her local twin group so she can go and meet other new mothers with twins, ideally before the babies arrive! This is particularly helpful if she is planning to breastfeed. She can speak to mothers who are breastfeeding twins for encouragement and inspiration before the babies are born.

> If babies have been in SCBU for a long time mothers will be happy and relieved to be at home, but may need extra reassurance as they have left the high dependency situation and are now 'on their own'. They may suffer from sudden exhaustion as they have been running on their nerves while in hospital and it can hit hard when home.

> As there is a high chance that one or both twins may need to spend time in SCBU it can be very traumatic to come home without one or both babies. The only advantage is that mothers can have time to get used to caring for one baby first! The downside is that the new parents will have to be travelling back and forth to divide their time between the babies.

> Babies may be more snuffly at home due to the change in atmosphere, as the home environment will be dryer and more dusty. There is no cause for concern as long as the babies are otherwise well. They are also at increased risk of infection, so only healthy visitors should be in contact, as respiratory infections are particularly danger-ous. The babies will also be less able to maintain their body temperatures and it is therefore im-portant to keep an eye on the tempera-ture of both room and babies. They are more likely to

have wind problems so encourage massage, more upright feeding, medium flow teats if bottle-feeding (rather than slow/newborn ones), warm baths, and medication of the mother's choice.

> There is an increased risk of postnatal depression in mothers of multiples, so be aware of mother's mental and physical state.

> The mother will need to eat an extra 500 calories per baby per day if breastfeeding.

> Babies coming home from SCBU may have medication, vitamins and iron supplements (even if they are breastfeeding). You may need to remind mothers to give these. In the last months of pregnancy babies store up vitamins, so if they are born before 36 weeks they may have missed out.

> Remind parents that they are on night duty and they *must* sleep at least once in the day, either while you are there or when both babies are hopefully asleep.

> As soon as you feel the mother is ready, encourage her to get out of the house, with your help. Coming out for the first time with a double buggy can be very daunting, so a gentle walk down the road is a great start!

> Suggest always allowing extra time for going out, as it is very common for complete strangers to stop you and expect you to have the time and patience to answer their perhaps well meaning, but often exasperating, questions. For example: Do twins run in your family? (None of your business!) Are they identical? (A boy and a girl? I don't think so!) And the most common and annoying: You must have your hands full! This is not helpful to an exhausted mum of twins. Strangers also often ask about the twins and totally ignore an older sibling.

> If possible encourage the mother/parents to take one or two babies out so they can have more focussed time with them as individuals, if they have someone to babysit

Ten great things about multiples

1. You have an instant family, just add milk.
2. If you get fed up with one, you always have the other.
3. Nobody asks if you are going to have any more children (at least for a year).
4. You never feel guilty about getting more help.
5. You get to eat 4,000 calories a day when breastfeeding (bring on the Haagen Dazs and Guinness).
6. Twins start giggling at each other as soon as they can smile.
7. You make proper use of buy-one-get-one-free offers at the Supermarket.
8. You only have to organise one birthday party a year.
9. You become a local celebrity in the cafés, park and playground.
10. Your twins will turn out to be more confident, supportive, innovative, giving, self knowing, and sought after than the average singleton.

Emma Mahoney, *Double Trouble*, 2003

the other/s. I saw this working very well in a triplet family I worked for.

> Premature babies may be sent home from hospital with an apnoea monitor. This piece of equipment records a baby's heart rate, breathing pattern, and sounds an alarm if the heart rate slows down or the baby stops breathing.

Breastfeeding twins

> Research breastfeeding positions for multiples. Remind the mother that there is no 'right' way to feed twins; support them as they try different ways until they find what works best for them and their babies.

> Encourage mothers to keep a feed chart with the time of feed, which baby, which breast and length of feed. Also they are encouraged to keep a track of nappy contents. Without this many mothers understandably lose track totally of when and who they last fed!

> Few preterm babies are fully breastfeeding when they come home from SCBU. It will take a huge amount of extra support and persistence on the mother's part, but most of these babies eventually breastfeed well. 'In the first six weeks mothers of multiples are less likely to stop than singleton mothers.' TAMBA

> Ensure the mother is totally comfortable and well fed and watered before she starts feeding.

> Ensure that each baby is feeding correctly before feeding them both together. This may take several weeks, but it is worth establishing feeding properly rather than having to

A twin mum's suggestions for making life easier with twins... finances permitting!

HELP. Cleaner, babysitter, doula or sensitive family member. Forget the fancy cot bumpers and matching clothes – get some help towards the end and for at least the first six months. We're not the kind of people who have 'help' but we got to three months and realised for the sake of our babies and our toddler – if we were to care for them properly, mum needed help. There's no shame in it. As soon as we acquiesced and got a babysitter for a couple of hours a day and a cleaner once a week, mum wasn't so overwhelmed and the babies and our son were happier by default.

Bunk bed cots. Expensive but cheaper than buying a new house. Sturdy and double as bunk beds until they're four years old. Can't fault them. (Normal cot bed sheets fit it).

Snuggle bundles. Bags to carry babies around, post caesarean, but also during that time when you can't let them out of your sight. They fall asleep in them and you can then easily transfer them to the car seat and back. Better then carrying two Cabriofix's because that's impossible after the first month. In fact don't bother with a travel system – they are for singletons. Choose a double pushchair for where you live. Travel systems are too much to deal with for twins and only useful for the first six months.

White noise on an MP3 recording, on an iPod in their room. This stops one waking the other and also calms them down. Good to put on for early mornings too.

Two *Jumperoos* – no two ways about it. When they can go in the Jumperoo, a whole new world of freedom opens up.

go back to correct 'bad' habits later.

> Fathers of twins are often very keen to 'help' with feeding. They need to understand that the milk supply and babies' latching should be established first, and that this will take at least six weeks. There will be plenty of time later to 'share' feeding, if the mother wants. There is a definite advantage for fathers of twins:

> 'With multiples dad has no choice but to be heavily involved in baby care. The only mothering task that dad can't do is breastfeed. Everything else can, and must, be shared by both parents if the whole family is to grow and thrive.' Sears, P. (p180)

> Assure a mother who plans to breastfeed that many women successfully breastfeed twins and that she can definitely produce enough milk to feed two babies.

> Encourage mothers to increase their confidence by speaking to other breastfeeding twin mums, either by joining local groups or online, *whilst still pregnant*! It is easier to make these connections before the babies arrive.

> Simultaneous feeding stimulates both breasts at once, which is *great* for increasing milk production.

> Alternate breasts in order to avoid one of them getting engorged if one of the babies is a more efficient feeder than the other.

> It is perfectly possible to produce ample milk for multiple babies as the system works on supply and demand. If twice as much milk is demanded, twice as much milk will be produced.

> Feed as early and often as possible after delivery to encourage lactation.

> If expressing, encourage the mother do this every two to three hours in the day and at least once at night, as prolactin levels are highest at night.

Triplets

Useful facts

> Average pregnancy length: 34 weeks.

> Average birth weight: 1.8kg.

> 92 per cent go to special care.

> C-section rate 95 per cent.

It is reported by Twins UK that it takes over 197 hours a week to care for triplets, so your help and the help of any others is vital for the new parents. All the strategies and tips for twins should be implemented plus:

> Be aware, prior to their delivery, of the increased complications triplets may have, such as prematurity, low birth weight, higher risk of abnormalities e.g. cerebral palsy.

> Before you start, encourage the family to make a weekly visiting schedule in advance so they know who is coming when and to ensure that not too many people come one week and no one the next. Also make sure the rota of help is coordinated so there is a balance of people who can help with feeds (most popular job!) and cook, clean, drive, etc.

> As well as family and friends and paid help, be aware of other free services such as Homestart (see Useful Contacts) and childcare students (contact local colleges).

> Discuss how the babies will be identified. The commonest way is to use a touch of nail polish on a finger nail.

> Suggest joining a multiples club and trying to contact another triplet family to meet before the triplets arrive.

> Encourage the use of a feed chart to keep pace with feeds.

> If possible encourage the mother/parents to take one or two babies out so they can have a more focussed time with them as individuals, if they have someone to babysit the other/s. I saw this working very well in a triplet family I worked for.

> As breastfeeding works by supply and demand it is totally possible to breastfeed triplets, but obviously not all at the same time but on a convenient rotation schedule.

Premature babies

Encourage skin-to-skin (kangaroo care) as this calms the baby, helps regulate breathing and heart rate, and favours breastfeeding. 'The mothers of premature babies produce more high fat colostrum, and for longer, to help their babies thrive.' Evans (p28)

> Premature babies' skin lacks the normal layers of fat and will appear thin, with veins and arteries visible. The skin may be red or purplish. It may take several weeks for the natural pigmentation to come through.

> Folded ears. Babies born more than six weeks early often have folded ears. The soft skin folds over because the strong cartilage which keeps them upright has not yet formed.

> Premature babies often don't move much because their muscles haven't yet developed to give them the needed strength. This improves over time as the baby gains weight and develops muscle mass.

> Premature babies have more 'active' sleep than term babies so will move around a lot more at night when they are home.

> Discharge from SCBU. If there are no problems, i.e. with feeding or weight gain, babies won't have to remain in hospital until their due date. Discharge at 37 weeks is the average.

> Babies will most likely come home on vitamin and iron supplements. Babies store up vitamins in the latter months of pregnancy so if they are born before 36 weeks they will have missed out on this.

> Breathing difficulties. Since the lungs aren't developed until the 28th week, babies born early often have difficulty breathing. If this is the case the baby will be placed on a ventilator and assisted with her breathing until her lungs develop further and are strong enough to support her system on their own.

> Some premature babies will go home with supplemental oxygen. This is delivered through nasal prongs and increases the amount of oxygen in the air that a baby breathes, without interfering with the baby's spontaneous breaths.

> Immunization and weaning are worked out according to birth date *not* corrected age.

> SCBU babies may get used to being on their tummies; sleeping on their back is usually introduced two weeks prior to discharge.

> Snuffly babies. The change from SCBU to the dryer and more dusty atmosphere at home can cause more snuffles, not colds.

> Increased risk of infection, especially if the babies have been ventilated, are very premature or have been on oxygen. Beware visitors!

> Low birth weight babies, below 5lb 8oz, can breastfeed as early as 28 weeks. Studies have shown that premature multiples mature more quickly than single babies born at a similar time. Multiples are often better equipped for an early start.

CHAPTER 8
Special situations

Postnatal Depression

Postnatal depression (PND) affects up to 15 per cent of new mothers, but this may not represent the full picture, as many women do not admit that they are suffering.

Mothers of multiples have twice the risk of postnatal depression.

PND is *not* a worse or lengthy case of the 'baby blues'. Postnatal depression will not go away without treatment, unlike the baby blues, which *will* pass. It does not always develop immediately following birth; it can occur up to a year later.

There are a number of reasons why a woman may develop postnatal depression. It can result from a combination of causes rather than a single trigger. Giving birth is a major life event that in itself can trigger a bout of depression. Other common factors include the following:

> Hormonal changes following delivery.

> Problems or complications during pregnancy or birth.

> Previous episodes or a family history of depression.
> Little or no support from family and/or friends.
> Marital problems or anxiety over money.
> Anxiety about the health of the baby.
> Exhaustion through lack of sleep from broken nights.
> Feeling overwhelmed by all the new responsibilities.
> Doubting her ability to be a 'good' mother.
> Suddenly losing the identity that she knew and struggling to come to terms with a new role where independence can be temporarily lost.

What are the symptoms?

> Depression.
> Mood swings.
> Low mood lasting a long time.
> Feeling alone.
> Feeling constantly tired and drained with low or no energy.
> Tension – headaches, stomach pains or blurred vision.
> Decrease in appetite or increased appetite.
> Reduced sex drive.
> Irritability, irrationally snapping.
> Feeling useless, worthless and guilty.
> Loss of interest or pleasure in relationships or surroundings.
> Panic attacks.
> Social phobia.
> Sleeping problems – unable to get to sleep or waking in the early hours and not being able to get back to sleep.
> Crying a lot, often over the smallest things or for no reason at all.
> Lack of motivation to do anything.

> Feeling overwhelmed by everything and unable to cope with the slightest demand.
> Constant feeling of anxiety.
> Unable to concentrate.
> No interest in the baby or not bonding.
> Overly anxious about the health of the baby.
> Not trusting anyone else with the baby.
> Irrational thoughts. *'My baby doesn't like me'*; *'Someone is going to steal my baby'*
> Thoughts of harming self or baby.

What can you do?

If you are a partner or regular helper/visitor you will be in a prime position to observe any relevant changes that may occur with a new mother, as you have the advantage of offering continuity of care. If possible you can implement many helpful strategies that can help prevent this situation from worsening.

> Provide a non-judgmental listening ear.
> Cook her a meal whenever possible. Also provide regular nutritional snacks – this is particularly important to keep blood sugar levels stable.
> Give the mother the opportunity to rest as much as possible, but at the same time be aware that 'taking the baby off' too much could be detrimental to her bonding with the baby.
> Encourage her to get out of the house for fresh air and a break as often as possible.
> If possible encourage any appropriate form of exercise, as this is known to release 'feel good' hormones.
> Do not try to help her 'shake it off' by trying to cheer her up, or suggesting she tries to snap out of it. If it has taken hold, this is not possible. Remember, she does not want to be like this, but may be feeling powerless under

the strength of the depression to fight it off.

> Be patient and accept that she will have good and bad days, as this can sometimes be the nature of postnatal depression. However some women are continuously depressed.

> Be aware that she may 'put on a show' of being alright, as she may feel guilty or that she has no reason to be depressed or be causing everyone so much worry.

> Buy her gifts or flowers.

> Prepare a bath for her and reassure her that she can have some time to herself while you look after the baby or other siblings.

> Give her hugs and cuddles, if accepted, but reassure her that you have no other physical agenda – newly delivered mothers can often feel extremely sensitive to physical advances too soon.

> Try not to take her reproaches and criticisms to heart. Loved ones usually snap at their nearest and dearest. She may well feel resentful that you have the freedom and ability to walk away if you choose, while she has the baby totally depending on her and cannot ever really switch off.

> Always refer to a professional if you have serious concerns.

I had a client with a history of postnatal depression with her second and third babies. In order to try and prevent a reoccurrence with her fourth child (more likely if you have had a previous episode) she implemented a support plan by booking me from day one to come every day with hours diminishing over a three-month period. The positive outcome for her and her family was that she did not suffer the postnatal depression again. Normal baby blues were identified, but passed with extra support.

Another client was having her second baby. She had a traumatic first birth, and her second birth was an

'When I walked up the stairs one day I was walking in mud, when I walked up the next day I was climbing through syrup. The next day the stairs had been replaced by Mount Everest and I struggled to get to the top. It sounds dramatic – but it's true.

My entire body ached continuously and every movement was an effort. Talking was a strain.

Everyday tasks such as clearing the table after breakfast became overwhelming and I did not know where to start, it was too complicated.

Noises were in stereo, headaches immense, no interest in food, feeling constantly sick, no vigour for life. Feeling displaced like a continuous out of body experience.

Major paranoia. I wouldn't leave the baby downstairs while I was upstairs in case someone came in the front door and took her. All doors would have to be locked.

Not sleeping for the fear of my baby dying in her sleep, continuously getting up and checking her breath.

One night I saw trickles of condensation dripping down the window. I imagined they were tears for my dead baby.

Holding my baby in my arms, wanting to just disappear with her in my arms, float away to a peaceful place.

Feeling like I have never felt happiness or will ever be happy. What's life all about?'

elective caesarean section. Once she came home from hospital and I came into the home, I witnessed a rapid deterioration within a matter of days. She became self-absorbed, preferred to be in a different room to the toddler and baby girl, couldn't switch off or sleep, started feeling paranoid that someone would steal the baby, and clearly had a distorted imagination. I spoke to the parents and suggested the mother should urgently see the GP that day.

She was immediately prescribed medication and referred for counselling. The medication took a few weeks to kick in but gradually Mum regained her equilibrium. I thought at the time that her condition could have spiralled quickly into puerperal psychosis. Mum had post-traumatic stress from her previous delivery, had recently moved house, her husband had a new job and they had moved away from friends and family. She was under an awful lot of strain. Mothers often don't realise just how much they are dealing with.

Postpartum psychosis

This is a more serious, and more rare, mental health condition that differs from postnatal depression. It affects just one or two women in every 1,000.

Symptoms usually appear in the first two weeks after the baby is born and include:

> Feeling depressed one moment and very happy the next; manic episodes.

> Severe confusion.

> Hallucinations: this can include hearing, smelling, seeing or feeling things that are not really there.

> Paranoia.

> Feeling like everything is a dream, disconnected from reality.

> Sleep problems, unable to sleep or wanting to sleep all the time.

> Believing things that are obviously untrue and illogical (delusions) – often relating to the baby, such as thinking the baby is dying, or that either you or the baby had magical powers.

> Seeing and hearing things that are not really there – this is often hearing voices telling you to harm the baby.

Postpartum psychosis is regarded as a psychiatric emergency. If you are concerned someone you know may have developed postpartum psychosis and you think there is a danger of imminent harm to the mother, her partner or her baby, call her doctor immediately. If it is outside the surgery's hours, call an ambulance or the local out-of-hours GP service.

Caesarean section
Emotional issues

If a mother has had a planned or elective caesarean section, for whatever reason, she will probably have had time to be prepared for and accepting of the situation. An unexpected or emergency casearean will obviously have a more serious impact on her recovery. She may experience a range of emotions ranging from disappointment, guilt and anger to feelings of inadequacy and that her body has 'failed her'. Encourage her to talk about her feelings if she feels comfortable to do so. If you feel this is not appropriate, suggest support groups such as Birth Crisis (see Useful Contacts). Encourage as much time holding and cuddling the baby as possible to help her to heal and bond. Your support can be valuable at this time, particularly in helping to find comfortable positions for feeding and resting, with the aid of extra cushions. Provide extra reassurance that this period of dependence won't last. Many mums find it really hard to stand back and watch others doing things for them. They may have ambivalent feelings towards you and all the fit and active people around them. But if a mum takes care now and recovers properly, she will be up and about quicker than if she pushes it too early. Encourage mothers to recognise and accept their temporary limitations and pace themselves.

Physical and practical tips

> Watch that the mother is not lifting shopping bags, laundry baskets, toddlers (a good idea is having a little step or box that the toddler can use to climb into her cot or bath) or trying to do strenuous exercise too soon.

> Make sure everything that is needed is in reach of the mum, as she will have restricted movement and mobility in the first few days and weeks.

> Suggest holding a pillow against her wound area when coughing, sneezing or laughing.

> Use a folded-up towel or bath mat over the bath side to protect her stomach whilst bathing the baby.

> Remind the mother to take pain relief medication regularly, if prescribed. Explain the importance of pain relief after a caesarean and warn her about the possibility of breakthrough pain. It's not a bravery contest!

> Painful wind and bloating can be a common symptom after a caesarean. This is caused by pockets of gas being trapped in the abdomen. Many women are not forewarned and can be taken aback by this. It can be very painful but is normal, and there may be referred pain as far as the shoulders. Peppermint oil or tea may be helpful.

> Be aware of any possible discomfort around the wound. If there is an increase in pain, or discharge, refer to midwife or GP.

> Make sure the mother is happy with the wound care instructions she has received (for example about bathing) and suggest she askes her midwife for any clarification that may be needed.

Babies with disabilities

'Children with disabilities have the same needs as every other child – to learn, play, be included, have friends and be loved by their parents. Whatever your child's disability, one of the most important things you can remember is to see your child as a child first and their disability as only a part of who your child is. As with any child, his or her future is influenced by the vision you hold for him or her and your commitment to realizing these dreams. As parents who have children with disabilities, our children have transformed our lives and taught us much about the value of family. We trust you will share in this experience."

One in 20 children in the UK is born with a disability. Even with today's advanced technology and the fact that we usually have prior knowledge of 'problems', new parents can never really be prepared for the shock/distress/reality of bringing home a baby with additional needs or a disability.

If you find yourself helping a family with a baby with a disability, it is important that you are as well informed and prepared as possible. The baby will probably have spent some time in a special care baby unit (SCBU). Parents will have been encouraged by SCBU nurses to be closely involved as soon as possible, thus helping increase their confidence. (You can learn now from the parents, by taking their lead.)

What can you do?

> Learn as much as possible about the condition before the baby arrives or prior to starting.

> Explore your own feelings and emotions... perhaps you have had a similar experience? It is important to keep your personal feelings 'in check'. Your role is to support and empathise, not 'share the despair'.

> Be aware of online help and support:

>> gov.uk/help-for-disabled-child/early-support-programme

>> bestbeginnings.org.uk/parents-with-learning-disabilities

>> cafamily.org.uk/

>> councilfordisabledchildren.org.uk

---

* See humanservices.alberta.ca/documents/DisabilitiesBook.pdf

It took us an unexpected 18 months to get pregnant with our second son. So when he was born at home, this perfect, long-awaited bundle, I couldn't believe my luck. I just kept staring at him. It got so strong, this feeling of having 'got something I didn't deserve', that I laughingly mentioned to a friend that I worried someone was going to knock on the door and take him away as he was too perfect. I wonder now if that obsession with 'being lucky' was some kind of sixth sense.

At the six-week check I mentioned to the doctor that he wasn't smiling or following me with his eyes. The doctor, a particularly old-school patronising chap, wrote in my notes 'plenty of smiles and eye contact'. After that I started to notice it more and more.

By eight weeks I had a horrible feeling something wasn't right with his eyes. They would slide around and not really fix on anything. There were still no smiles. I had a sense of dread and I became so worried so quickly that I couldn't even tell my husband. I thought if I said it out loud it would be true.

A week later I walked in to a room unexpectedly to find my husband staring at our baby and waving a hand in front of his face. I realised he had noticed it too. We went back to the doctor's the next day and within 24 hours we were sat in a consultant's office receiving devastating news.

The consultant checked my son over and asked us to wait outside. My heart sank. You don't ask someone to wait outside to tell them nothing is wrong. When he called us back in he told us that he had three theories – two of them meant permanent blindness and one of them meant brain surgery with limited life-expectancy. We were to go to Great Ormond Street Hospital the next day for further tests.

I don't remember the journey home, or the evening. What I do remember is lying next to my baby whilst he slept and silently crying like I had never cried before. In amongst my tears I told my baby, out loud, that whatever was wrong with him, I would love him and protect him forever. I know we all make that promise to our children, but this came from a deeper, angrier place than even us mummies usually go.

I'm ashamed to say I was to break that promise within the week. When the diagnosis came, it brought with it a horrible numbing sensation. We were told by phone on a Sunday, just as we arrived at a large family gathering, that our son was severely visually impaired – he would be registered as blind, he would never see colour and never be able to stand bright sunlight. He wouldn't need brain surgery and he would live, but I'm afraid it seemed little consolation. My husband and I had to endure the family party without saying a word.

For the next week I felt numb and totally disconnected from my baby. I am so ashamed to admit this now. But it's important for me to share just how gritty this situation can get. I spent hours imagining the worst possible life for us, without any emotion whatsoever.

We finally met with the consultant who shared more details with us and we had to tell our family and friends. In my numbness I sent a very business-like e-mail informing them of the diagnosis and telling them how to behave (they were not allowed to call me in tears, give me examples of successful blind musicians or give me a list of reasons to feel positive). For the most part, my close family were great. They said and did the right things. But then the cards started to come. I hated them. I felt like instead of saying 'sorry to hear your news' they were actually saying 'thank God it's you and not us'. Several people turned up on the doorstep with gifts for us! I was so angry at the world I threw them all in the bin.

But gradually, that fierce, protective mummy who had made a promise fought her way through the pain and came to the surface. I'm glad to say it didn't take her long, a fortnight, maybe a few days more. I had a realisation one day that the reason I had taken so long to get pregnant was that, when he came, I would be so grateful for him that it would give me the strength to cope with this change of plan.

You might think that sounds a bit crazy, but it has got me through the hardest times, the thought that I was chosen for this very special task. I know there are parents out there who get much worse news than we did, but that is very little comfort.

Why would it make me feel better that there are parents worse off than us? That just makes me feel even sadder that anyone has to go through anything like this.

I'm not sure I have many 'tips' to give: we're all so different, aren't we? I wouldn't send a card and I definitely wouldn't show up with a gift. The best gift you can give a mother is to love her baby, hold her baby like he is the most perfect thing in the world and look after them until her 'Tiger' mummy emerges. Listen to her if she wants to talk, but don't share her emotion: you can't and you don't really have the right. Save your own tears for another time. Don't tell her to 'be positive' or give any other instruction. Just follow her lead.

My younger son is now nearly five years old. Both our sons are the light of our lives. But he is just a little bit special in so many ways. He has brought us nothing but positivity and good experiences. He made us stronger as a family and we all found our protective side. If you know the joy of seeing your baby take his first steps, you need to double it for a child who has come

> through challenges. Every time they prove someone wrong your heart grows a size bigger. It's an amazing feeling and I feel blessed for being given the chance to feel it.
> This morning it was his first day back at school since the Christmas holidays. He was a little nervous getting ready so asked if it would be okay if he wore his Ninja mask for the journey to school. When we got to the front door he leapt out of the house and shouted 'I am ready to face my destiny', before executing a few choice ninja moves and climbing in to the car. This, I think, tells you all you need to know about where I draw my strength from these days.

Mothers with disabilities

Learning disabilities

'Around 40% of parents with a learning disability do not live with their children. The children of parents with a learning disability are more likely than any other group of children to be removed from their parents' care.'[*]

The babies of mothers with learning disabilities are at increased risk of poor birth outcomes, including: premature birth (28 per cent) and low birthweight (22 per cent).

Antenatal education is vital for parents with a learning disability who may find themselves having their parental competence assessed soon after birth by social workers, before they have had time to develop and practice their skills and confidence as parents.[**]

Visual impairment

Gemma Edwards, a mum of two, now aged thirteen and seven, has been totally blind all her life. She's a doula and antenatal teacher, specialising in working with visually impaired parents. She's also co-founder of Blind Mums Connect, a rapidly growing organisation which supports visually impaired (VI) mums across the UK. She draws not only on her personal experiences, but also her experience of supporting and chatting to dozens of new parents over the years.

[*] See www.bestbeginnings.org.uk/parents-with-learning-disabilities
[**] See www.changepeople.org/resources for learning 1 to 5

The first thing to say to those supporting visually impaired mums and dads is that we share the same worries as all new parents. We may feel overwhelmed by being suddenly responsible for a dependent little person, anxious about our ability to breastfeed or ensure our baby is thriving, panicky about how we will soothe and settle our baby once left alone through long wakeful nights. At the same time, we face all the challenges that other parents do, such as adjusting to a new lifestyle and lack of sleep!

That said, visually impaired parents face some particular challenges when it comes to the practicalities of every day babycare, as well as dealing with the attitudes of those around us. (For more about VI parenting, see Appendix 4).

Deafness

Clearly, if you are a supporting a relation or friend with a new baby you will have had experience of how to communicate with them. However, if this is your first encounter/engagement you will need some helpful tips. The most commonly suggested are:

DO
> Keep eye contact while communicating.
> Speak at a normal volume.
> Use a pen and paper if necessary.
> Check that they have understood and repeat if necessary.
> Use gestures and visual clues.

DON'T
> Shout or exaggerate your mouthing, as this will only distort the lips.
> Don't assume deaf people are not intelligent!
> Don't presume that all deaf people can sign.

For more information, see www.deafparent.org.uk/links.php

Supporting parents with physical disabilities

Sue Saunders is a doula who has worked with families with physical disabilities. Her comments, although relating to doula support, are useful for anyone who may be supporting families with physical disabilities.

The first point I would like to make is that doulaing for a family with a parent who has a disability is the same as any other doula job – unique, while at the same time being very similar to all other doula jobs.

Many parents with disabilities may not have had enthusiastic support for their pregnancy from their families, and as a doula you must remember they are parents first. They may not be able, for example, to change a nappy the same way as you, but their way is no less valid. Many parents with disabilities choose to have a doula as it is support for parenting, not for their disability. Disability support rarely takes into account a parenting role, and may even suggest or demand that the non-disabled partner assumes the child carer role, while the disabled parent is expected to watch from the sidelines.

As with any doula job it is important to build a rapport with the family, and ask what they want from you as a doula. It's important here to recognise that parents with disability may choose to do all aspects of parenting – perhaps slower than you are used to seeing and you may be tempted to jump in. They may choose to oversee some of the more practical aspects of parenting, such as nappy changes, and save their energy for the more nurturing things. Either way, you take your lead from the family. Only in an emergency situation should you be taking a carer role, for example an older child running into the road or baby starts to roll on changing table and your job is to make baby safe.

For example: B was able to change D's nappy but chose to have her doula C change them when she was there as B wished to save her energy to play with D. C notices that D has soiled his nappy. C says 'I think D's had a poo, do you want to check?' B chooses to check and asks C to change the nappy, C notices a little nappy rash and draws B's attention to it and follows B's lead. Doula C has remembered B is still the parent and is acting as B's hands and eyes only.

Y was very nervous about taking baby out of the house on her own. As a wheelchair user she had an adapted buggy which attached to her wheelchair. Doula S accompanied her on visits to the Children's Centre and supermarket until Y was confident that she could access the premises with baby and, in the case of the Children's Centre, the staff and parents had got to know her and the baby and were willing to help if needed. Again here it is important for the doula to remember their role and for example not give details about the baby e.g. 'Ahhh is it a boy or girl?' 'Y, I think this lady is talking to you.'

I was working for a family where both parents were full-time wheelchair users. In our interview we discussed their abilities and what they felt they needed help with. We discussed the boundaries of my role and how they imagined that I would be of assistance. Mum and dad both wanted to take part in floor play with baby – which we knew would be impossible due to them being unable to get off the floor without help. We were able to think about this as a team and with the aid of some bed guards they were able to move floor play to their double bed and play there. We had built up our relationship whereby they were able to actively take part in all aspects of parenting. I was unable to extend my doula placement with them but I actively helped them to look for an appropriate carer for when I finished, as my presence had helped them to see what they could do and how they could be supported.

Bereavement

Seventeen babies die shortly after birth or are stillborn every day in the UK.* SIDS (Sudden Infant Death Syndrome, often referred to as 'cot death') affects around 290 babies every year in the UK. These statistics illustrate that that there is always a possibility that you could be involved with a family following the tragic death of a baby.

If you have offered support, your role will clearly no longer be needed in the same way. However, as a postnatal doula, family member or friend you will still be well-placed to support the bereaved parents emotionally and practically if they wish. Practical help will be invaluable, providing food and helping with arrangements.

Be aware/mindful of your personal history. If you have suffered a loss yourself it can well bring back those feelings of grief. Ensure you have immediate support if this happens. If you have been thinking about working as a postnatal doula, you may already have addressed and 'cleared' the issue prior to commencing work as a doula.)

If one or more multiples dies, be aware that the most common response 'Oh well, at least you still have the other(s)' is of no comfort to the parents, who will be trying to process both grief and joy.

As well as encouraging parents to get immediate support it is essential for you to get the support you need. FSID will speak to professionals and carers alike. See Useful Contacts for the helpline number. Doula UK are in the process of setting up a bereavement course for doulas.

If you are supporting a mother who has just given birth, she will of course need all the emotional help you can give, and indeed practical help. If she is lactating she may be prescribed medication to stop this, or she may choose to donate her milk to a breast milk bank (see Chapter 6).

---

* See www.uk-sands.org/about-us/aims-and-objectives/our-impact

CHAPTER 9
A career as a postnatal doula

|f this book has inspired you, or if you have supported families informally already and are keen to do more, you might give serious thought to becoming a postnatal doula. It can be a rich and varied job, but it is not for everyone and you will need to think carefully about whether you have the right personal characteristics. This chapter gives more information about the day-to-day reality of working as a postnatal doula to help you decide on your own path.

The 'package of care' that you offer will vary depending on your experience, availability and the needs of the mother.

Examples of a typical doula day

1. 'Easy' day

First baby, eight days old

10am	Arrive
10–10.30am	Listen to the activities of the last 24 hours e.g. feeds, sleep etc. Ascertain the needs and priority for the day. If this is not clear ask what the mother most needs help with today.
10.30am	Baby wakes up and has a breastfeed. Prepare and give smoothie to mum. Empty and load dishwasher. Wipe down surfaces.

10.45am	Suggest mum goes to bed for a rest. Some mothers are resistant and will insist they are not tired. No problem, suggest they take time out to shower, lie down and read… don't force it. Many times they think they are not tired because of adrenaline, but in fact are asleep minutes later. Meanwhile wind the baby, change nappy and give nappy-free kicking time or tummy time. Suggest mum provides some old towels for this.
11.30am	Swaddle and settle baby. Make soup for lunch, fold laundry, and refresh flowers.
12.45pm	Baby wakes hungry for feed. Take baby to mum in bed. Discuss how she is and leave in peace.

2. 'Challenging' day

Toddler, 2½ years old, and baby, eight days old

10am	Arrive. Mum in tears in dressing gown. Screaming toddler clinging to her leg with smelly full nappy. Baby screaming in arms, has been feeding off and on all night. Food delivery being delivered to kitchen. Cat sick on the floor. Porridge boiling over on the stove.

Take screaming baby. Suggest mother goes upstairs with toddler to do nappy and has a shower. Hand her a drink and toddler a snack to keep her distracted while mother is in the shower.

Meanwhile baby still fractious (overtired?) Carry her round to calm her whilst putting frozen stuff away. Put baby in chair and sort out porridge. Gloved up, clean sick before toddler comes back. Answer door and ward off unexpected visitors. Make breastfeeding tea.

10.45am   Mum comes down. Baby desperate for breast. Settle her with baby, cushions and tea. Baby feeds then falls asleep.

Distract toddler.

11.15am   Midwife arrives. Has to wake baby to weigh, she screams again. Toddler gets upset, knocks over drinks, cries and bites mum.

11.45am   Midwife leaves. Suggest mum lies on settee to feed baby, cuddle and read a story to toddler. Meanwhile clear kitchen, finish putting shopping away, sort laundry. Make pasta salad for lunch.

Before you start: the reality!

In order to embark on this career path I suggest you consider the following points and take time to reflect honestly.

> Can I keep my life in balance? Keep up with my family, home life, running the home, time with children, time for pleasure? How much time can I realistically give?

> If I commit certain hours to my client, am I compromising my own family and home life? I have often heard postnatal doulas say. 'I spent two hours playing Lego with the toddler when my own child was at the childminder, which of course I have to pay for. I spent two hours ironing, which really annoyed me knowing I had a huge pile of my own at home. I cooked the most amazing meal, which I left for the family to enjoy and then had to come home to nothing prepared!' It is clearly important to avoid this kind of resentful situation. Some doulas will actually choose not to take on jobs where there are older siblings.

> Are you prepared to be and can you be discreet and confidential? You are not there to discuss your personal life or problems. You are there for your client exclusively and must not discuss other clients.

> As you are a 'carer', make sure you get replenished too! Can you maintain some level of 'detachment' and avoid being like a sponge: absorbing others' problems and taking them home? Have you got a way to relax and debrief? Make sure you have a fellow doula you can talk to.

'I would do almost anything for my clients, but I would say the most important part is listening to them just chattering away whilst I get on with other things. We are so privileged and like hairdressers and other therapists we are a "safe ear". I know immensely personal things about most of them: I listen and it goes no further.'

> Am I happy working alone? If you are used to working in a team or alongside others you may find yourself feeling isolated. It can be quite a 'lonely' job. It is a good idea, therefore, to network and find other doulas who you feel you could call on in your area, not forgetting, of course, that you can always call on your doula mentor. Ensure that you have a good relationship with her as she is, as it were, your doula throughout the process of your doula journey. Her support and guidance will be invaluable. Birth doulas nearly always have back up and are therefore more likely to have closer and more regular doula contact.

> Am I reasonably fit? Lifting can take its toll on weak backs. Are you ok on your feet for long hours? Do you catch everything? You will be exposed to the bugs that babies and small children inevitably get.

> We are often 'everything' to our clients: they have no other support. I believe it is my responsibility to keep as fit as possible so that I won't let them down. It is also clearly important not to work when unwell, to avoid exposing your client and new baby to infection. Equally you should avoid attending a family who are infectious. Obviously this is sometimes unavoidable and we will be ill or have a family crisis that we will be committed to deal

with and feel very torn. This highlights the suggestion of (where possible) having a local doula that you would feel confident in suggesting for back up. This is always easier if you have met and trust this doula and feel she works in a compatible way so you feel confident and comfortable in sharing the job if necessary.

> Am I prepared to be flexible, within reason, in my work schedule? Start and finish dates rarely go as planned where birth is concerned. Also, can you offer early starts or late finishes, or be prepared to stay on in an emergency?

> The reason some doulas chose to only do postnatal work is that they don't want to be on call and like to be able to plan ahead. It can be helpful to know on Monday that I am working four mornings, or whatever, that week.

> Am I prepared to drive long distances? Be clear on your limits as endless driving can be tiring. Also remember that although you may charge mileage you do not charge 'driving time'.

> Are you able to be open and non-judgmental about various parenting styles? Consider Gina Ford (strict routines), and Attachment Parenting/Continuum Concept-style.

> Would you be prepared to support a family with things that you may feel uncomfortable about or be unfamiliar with? For example: parents who smoke in their home, are of another culture/religion to you, who perform

circumcision or eat the placenta... would you be happy to prepare a placenta smoothie? It is crucial to be non-judgmental, so be clear on this prior to committing to a job.*

> Are you prepared to work in homes with certain pets? Perhaps you are allergic to cats or have a fear of dogs.

Some other points to consider

> Time-keeping: your visit is very important to the mother. If you are always on time the mother will trust that you are reliable. If she is having problems she will feel reassured that help will soon be at hand.

> Being a doula is a continuous learning process. The knowledge attained is never comprehensive, complete or conclusive as each and every job brings new and different challenges and requires renewed flexibility.

> Plan your breaks and holidays well in advance. If you do it will be easier to be selective about the jobs you choose to do. Although it is great to be in demand, be wary of taking on too many jobs at once. Two at a time is usually manageable, depending on the hours. Cramming too much in can be exhausting and quickly lead to burn out and you do not want to 'short change' your clients.

> Network in your community so you have a comprehensive list of professionals to refer your clients to. It is also helpful to know the timetables or whereabouts of local mother and baby activity groups to recommend.

---

* See **placentanetwork.com/your-placenta** and **thegreenparent.co.uk/articles/read/reclaiming-the-placenta**

'BEWARE of putting on the 'expert' hat! It's tempting to feel flattered when asked a question. Too easy to eagerly jump in with the answer. The wise doula will listen, wait, watch for signs and maybe reflect back to the woman. A woman's 'gut' feelings about most situations are the right ones.

She may just need to voice her thoughts and share with someone who is interested, not emotionally involved and who has an accumulated collection of varied different aspects and issues on birth and parenting.

A good answer is always, 'I'm sorry, I don't know the answer to that, but I know someone who does!'

Are you ready?

Attending a doula course is really only the first step on your path to becoming a doula. It is vital to check your knowledge base prior to starting work. Consider taking other courses to enhance your knowledge and volunteering in relevant settings to extend your experience.

I felt it would be valuable for postnatal doulas to provide the following helpful information for new trainees before they start out. To this end I devised a survey, which is reproduced here with a selection of answers. 3/4 of the respondents said they wished they had been better prepared to provide breastfeeding support with more in depth or further training.

What do you wish you had known or done before you started working as a postnatal doula?

> I think all doulas should do further studying in breastfeeding as we are fortunate enough to be with a woman right from the start and can do a great deal to help make it work.

> It is essential to have had some training in breastfeeding and to have a list of breastfeeding counsellors or lactation consultants that you can refer women to.

> Attend a paediatric first aid course. Would you know what to do in a medical emergency? All parents will be reassured to know that you have attended a paediatric first aid course. And you will feel more confident should an emergency arise.

> That being is more important than doing!

> What to expect in terms of development for newborns – what's normal/what's not.

> I wish I'd known that women can't predict how long they will need a doula for. I'd have had a much more flexible contract from the beginning.

> How important it is to develop a relationship with the client so they see you as emotional support as well as practical support from day one.

> Communication skills are very important – when to keep quiet, when not to!

> It's really important to understand the importance of being still and listening as we often assume that we have to do lots of useful tasks – we also just need to listen and give emotional support.

My further suggestions are:

> Familiarise yourself with how baby equipment is assembled. You will often need to assist in the setting up of buggies, car seats, travel cots, breast pumps, sterilizers, monitors etc. A trip to a large baby equipment store where you can be shown would be very helpful!

> Care of multiples: attend a course, read up for plenty of information, speak to other doulas who have twin experience.

> Be aware of the importance of keeping up your own Continuous Professional Development once you have started, as this is essential and in fact a requirement (of Doula UK)

> Regularly update your baby care knowledge as guidelines

frequently change and can therefore become outdated. Examples include making up infant formula, storing breast milk and nutrition.

> Volunteer in a local breastfeeding café, Children's Centre, or postnatal ward.

Let's go!
First impressions

When you get an initial phone enquiry make sure you are positive and articulate. If it is not a good moment always apologise and suggest another time to speak. As soon as you get an email enquiry always reply promptly. (Check your spam folder regularly.)

Be clear about your availability. Occasionally you may get an enquiry asking for help outside your normal work: 'Can you collect children from school, or do the housework while I go to the gym?' Clarify here what it is that they are really looking for, a cleaner, childminder or postnatal doula?

Interview

As with most interviews first impressions are usually what count. Most people can tell pretty soon if they like you. It is worth reading the questions that clients are recommended to ask (see Appendix 1) at interviews and be clear on your answers. Your job as a doula will be a very personal and close relationship with the mother and it is vital that you 'click'. Clarify what to do if things don't work on either side by having a trial period and appropriate exit strategy. Encourage your client to take her time to make her decision and also suggest she meets other doulas. This may, in effect, seem like you are doing yourself out of a job, but it is more important that she feels that her choice is right for her. You need to feel that it's right for you too.

Explain the typical pattern of hours to expect. It is best to negotiate and clarify the hours that are required before you start. It is advisable to book fewer sessions with the possibility of extending rather than lots over many weeks and then finding she doesn't need you.

If she does not decide on the spot, always give a day that you need to know by. Otherwise you can be left 'hanging on' and possibly jeopardising your chance of finding other work at that time.

Do encourage potential clients to follow up references via phone or email.

Pre-start visit

Once the client has confirmed the booking, I suggest doing a pre-start visit about a month before she is due. (This will, of course, depend on when you get your booking). I do not charge for this. This creates the opportunity to get to know the family better and to be shown around the house. You don't want to be bothering the mum on day one with questions like 'Where are the tea bags?' and 'How does the washing machine work?'

The following are other useful points to cover:

> Ascertain the kind of support they anticipate they will need.

> Feeding. If you are not booked to start immediately after the birth it is a good idea to check in over the phone to see how things are going. At this point, if there is a problem and things are not straightforward you can make suggestions and/or point them in the direction for appropriate help. It is far better to do this than to try to 'fix' things two weeks or more down the line when the feeding problems could have escalated.

> Give a short overview of what to expect in the first few weeks. If it's their first baby, pre-warn them about the realities of recovery. Even after a normal birth mothers may experience tiredness and soreness, pain when breastfeeding and after pains.

> Ideally meet all the family members and pets.

> Ask about any cultural traditions or rituals, dietary preferences, allergies and so on. Make suggestions about ingredients to have in (if appropriate). Some mums are keen to be provided with a list of ingredients which they can buy before I start. I also offer, as an alternative, to buy what is needed and then be reimbursed. I also say that I am always happy to pick up last-minute items.

> Ask for GP, postnatal ward and midwife phone numbers, in case of an emergency.

> Check the location of a First Aid box or equipment, particularly if you will be responsible for other children.

> Ask if there are particular ways she does or doesn't like things done around the house. Is there any particular chore that she wishes to retain for herself, to keep her feeling 'in control'?

> Pets. Some people are perfectly happy for their pets to roam the kitchen surfaces; others are not.

> Ask the client what their main concerns are.

> Explain that you will naturally take the initiative and do what needs doing. Some mothers, however, like to prepare a list of chores and questions in advance. This is helpful if they have an issue with asking for help. It is great if you can tick everything off at the end of your visit!

> Reassure them that their confidentiality will be respected.

> Tell them that they don't need to be up and dressed to let you in. Some new mothers try to impress me by being dressed and fully made up for the first few days or weeks, which thankfully soon fades into the relief of them greeting me in their dressing gown and being more themselves. Some clients give me a key so as to avoid disturbing them if feeding or sleeping.

> Make suggestions about postnatal remedies such as

Rescue Remedy, Arnica, Lavender oil, Floradix, Spatone (iron tonics).

> Equipment: mothers often want to 'check' with you if they have the 'right' equipment. Obviously this is a personal thing governed by individual financial situations. Where appropriate suggest second-hand equipment from Freecycle, Mumsnet etc.

> Cat net – also protects from bugs, bees. Proper cat nets do not protect from bugs as they have a really wide mesh so that the cat won't like treading on it. Determined cats will sit on bug nets so keep a close eye.

> Baby scissors. Some mums are nervous about cutting nails at first. Only offer to show them if you are confident and experienced. It is far easier to do when the baby is asleep. Many mothers prefer to nibble their babies' nails to avoid accidents! Emery boards are good too.

> It is useful to have lots of muslins and/or old towels. A baby bath is not essential; a sink or washing-up bowl will suffice. Changing mat not essential. No need for expensive changing station. Only cotton wool and water needed in first weeks. No creams necessary to start with.

First day

Be aware that you are entering a space and time that is unique and precious. There can be a beautiful atmosphere around a new baby. The mother and baby are 'charged' with the feel good hormone oxytocin. We need to respect, honour and help to maintain and preserve this calm. Speak softly and try to protect the family from intrusion; such as too many visitors or phone calls.

In contrast you may enter a scene of chaos and confusion and tension!

Be aware that the parents may be in a state of shock. They could be facing a huge and often daunting learning curve. They will need time to process what has happened during and since the birth. Allow them time together and

'I started the job four days after taking the phone call, despite the fact that I was overseas at the time. Doing live-in work has its challenges, and I live in Spain when I am not working, so on some occasions, like this one, I arrive at a job having simply chatted with the family a couple of times, and I haven't had the chance to meet them, so I've no idea what the setup is, or the standard of accommodation I will enjoy, until I arrive. By then I have a signed contract and have a deposit of one week's fee in the bank, so I can't really back out of the job, whatever surprises I find!

'When I arrived, Mum opened the door and it was immediately apparent that she was exhausted. Her daughter was perched on her shoulder, her face was bright red and she was screaming her head off, and waving her arms and legs about frantically. "She's like this most of the time she's awake", said Mum. I nearly turned on my heels and ran back to the car, but I thought that wouldn't be very professional, so I took a deep breath, and stepped over the threshold. I had only been trained to be a doula four months earlier when I took on this job, and I hoped that I would be up to the challenge!'

give them the opportunity if they wish to talk through the birth process with you. If they do not want to talk, it can be helpful to suggest that they write about their feelings.

After your first two sessions it is a good idea to ask the mother if she is happy with how things are going. Check whether she would like you to be doing anything differently.

Practical considerations and personal presentation

> Whether you wear jeans or not is up to you but some people I feel would not 'approve', so I wear a skirt or

casual trousers. I don't ever wear jogging bottoms or track suits. Sometimes this can be a messy job, so I always carry spare clothes in the car in case of any spillage. I do, however always arm myself with a muslin over my shoulder, chest or knees when handling the baby. They can be very unpredictable from either end!

> Always wash your hands immediately on arrival so that your client will be reassured. And always following nappy changing. Keep a hand sanitiser on you at all times so you can apply whenever necessary, particularly if in a hurry, and beware of cross infection if you go from one job to another on the same day.

> Avoid wearing overpowering scent. A new mum doesn't want her baby handed back to her smelling of you.

> Personal hygiene is important as you will get physically close i.e. bending close to observe/help with breastfeeding. Tying back long hair is also a good idea.

> Keep nails from catching on delicate baby skin.

> Avoid protruding rings, bracelets, watches or necklaces as they can easily catch or harm babies' skin.

> No itchy or scratchy fabrics. No fabrics that could shed or moult on the baby, such as mohair.

> Bring your own apron (if you use one) and slippers or indoor shoes that you can leave at the house for the duration of the job. Supportive indoor footwear is a particularly good idea as you can be on your feet for a long time.

Extra tips and ideas suggested by postnatal doulas

The following is a survey I conducted with the following question:

Can you share the top tips that you have found useful in your practice as a postnatal doula, which may be useful to those just starting out?

> Be as flexible as possible. Be willing to put your hand to a wide range of domestic duties as every family's needs are different. Have a sense of humour!

> Be very clear on your boundaries from the beginning. Be flexible but not a push-over. Look after/ask after the well-being of other household members too (including pets!)

> Listen carefully – not necessarily just the spoken word. Leave your own beliefs and parenting choices at the door – don't talk about yourself or what you'd do. Be as flexible as you can without losing out – new mums are always all over the place!!...?

> Get mum to write a list of what she would like done, or suggestions, a good starting point. Loads of encouragement and praise, especially for first-time mums.

> Be prepared to listen. Be prepared to fit in. Be prepared to leave your comfort zone.

> Network with other doulas/health professionals. Empower the mother. You are not a maternity nurse to take her baby away from her.

> Let the mother talk, talk, talk... Reassure her that she is doing a great job. Boost her confidence at every opportunity.

> Spend time with the mum before the birth to get an understanding of what she expects. Listen reflectively and don't judge her choices (as long as she has had access to up-to-date information). Continue to remind her how important it is for her to look after herself – sleep, food, fresh air, time out.

> When I start a new job, this is my order of priorities: 1. Listening – make a cup of tea for both of us and sit down to listen to the woman – her birth story, how she is feeling, what her needs are. In subsequent visits I do the same – sometimes it is a quick chat, sometimes it is much more in-depth. Sometimes the more in-depth talks happen later on and different emotions surface. Don't forget to

tell mum what a great job she did birthing her baby and how amazing she is now, caring for her baby. 2. Has mum eaten/had sufficient to drink. She may need to be reminded to have a glass of water near her when she feeds. 3. How is feeding going – do we need to think about this/ spend some time on this. 4. Is there a meal prepared for lunch and supper? 5. Is the laundry sorted? 6. Has mum had a sleep/rest – can I look after the baby/take the baby out for a walk whilst mum sleeps? (Can I do any shopping/ errands whilst out?) 7. Emptying the dishwasher, cleaning etc happens if everything else is done.

> Learning how to support couples in the use of slings! Biological nurturing techniques to help get BF off to a good start/help solve problems. Understanding that 'less is more'. It's not always about the housework, but about remembering that PN doulas should have two ears, two eyes and one mouth!

> Use a contract – only do what you are happy to do – agree set times early on.

> Housework: 'I'm happy to do pretty much anything cleaning-wise really. I would rather clean than cook and have to say I've not been asked to cook yet, thank goodness! I've done ironing, sweeping/mopping floors, putting on a washing, taking it out and hanging up or loading the tumble, I've cleaned the bathrooms, cleaned kids bedrooms, wiped down surfaces, polished, loaded the dishwasher and washed the things that can't go in the dishwasher. I've even cleaned the loos! If, however, I felt I was doing everything while the client was doing nothing for herself then I'd start doing less and less, but the clients I've done this for have also been more than happy to hand me the baby and get on with housework themselves 'for a break from baby'. One of my clients used to spend a fair bit of time online or reading glossy magazines, but usually when she did this she'd hand me baby so all I had to do was cuddle him and she'd chat while she was reading or

whatever. I really don't mind what they need from me if it's helping them settle into their new family life, as long as me being there is benefitting them and not allowing them to rely on me then I'm easy.'

> ...don't try too hard, by which I mean, by just being present, you bring so much to a postnatal family.

> 'Two weeks before Christmas, three to four hours, three days a week, mum late 20s, quite private, motherhood not really coming that naturally to her, babe now three weeks old, cleaner, immaculate house, one hour left on the last day (23 December) and she was feeding and having a nice time with her baby and chatting at that moment didn't feel the right thing. I did ask her because I really had done everything my initiative would allow, "Shall I iron those shirts?"

"What I'd really like you to do is play with the cat". A year-old pedigree, whose nose was well out of joint because of the baby. So I spent an hour chucking plastic golf balls round the big basement kitchen!'

> But as has already been said SO much depends on who and how everyone is. For some clients, I would do anything I would consider doing for my own children and their partners, including sitting and reading or cleaning a loo if necessary and for others a much more reserved and prescribed approach, just as one client might need a cuddle and big hugs when you say goodbye and others just a hand on their arm or shoulder to wish them well. To some we end up almost being a member of the family and with others you definitely feel like the paid help.'

'What do postnatal doulas do when everything is done? The washing is done, the mum is fed, the baby is asleep and you still have two hours left?' *Question from a postnatal doula on a doula forum.*

> Make a batch of soup or something for the freezer when you might not be there.

> Suggest leaving rather than hanging about to get paid for doing nothing and suggest staying longer on another day when needed.

> Ask them if they would like to chat about anything we haven't had time to cover in previous visits.

Crossing the boundary from doula to friend

Occasionally you may have a client who wants to meet up again once your working time is over. It could be for coffee and to have a baby chat and catch up. You need to be clear about where you choose to stand: whether to continue as a friend or keep the relationship purely professional.

Often you will be invited to attend christenings, naming ceremonies, birthdays and so on. Again, be clear about your relationship. Of course it is an honour that they wish to include you. However, if you say yes to every invitation you could be extremely busy socially.

Closure

Typically the time spent for singletons would be six to eight weeks. With twins it is more likely to be up to three months and with triplets even longer.

Before you leave it is important to revisit initial worries and confirm positively what the mum has achieved: she is confident bathing the baby, happy with feeding, and has managed to get out of the house, and so on.

I usually do a gradual decrease from four weekly sessions, to three, then two and then just one. This works really well so they don't find themselves suddenly on their own. Remember that you are there to support them so that they are coping well and are 'good to go' by the time you leave. I always reassure them that although I may be with other clients, I am always happy for them to contact me again if they need extra support. They may need me for an emergency bad day or possibly to babysit, which some doulas may be happy to do. It is always good for them to know this, particularly as you will most likely have forged closeness and you know them, their family and their home well. It is also nice for the mothers if you call a week later after finishing, checking in and seeing how things are going.

One client with twins told me on the last day: 'When you said I would be fine by three months I could not believe it, but now I know you were absolutely right.'

Ensure that you have provided or introduced all local follow-up contacts, such as Homestart, local mother and baby groups etc. It is well worth the time and effort to get to know your local practitioners of cranial osteopathy, yoga and so on so you feel happy and confident in recommending them and in turn they will be positive and confident to recommend you.

There is a noticeable difference between the nature of support that you provide at the start of a job to the role that you have when it is clearly time to move on. The feeling is that your assistance is more like a 'home help' as you will now be doing more household chores and less of the full on emotional and practical support. This transition is a good and positive sign that your work is done and that mum is fine and confident in her own skills and handling all the baby issues.

'I see a totally pale, exhausted looking mother with dark shadows under her eyes, who miraculously has the energy to sing and rock her baby in a way that he is starting to recognize. I see him relax, and his tense body seems to melt into her arms. He isn't crying now. His whole body is attentive to the music and wonderful rhythm of the mother who is comforting him so well. It takes a long time until he finally reaches sleep. When he does, the entire room seems at peace. Something momentous seems to have changed. It has been a journey, a transition from distress into harmony. The mother looks up with a warm smile. The miracle was hers, but perhaps you and I helped her by being there and seeing what she did as "something".'

What Mothers Do: especially when it looks like nothing

Naomi Stadlen

POSTSCRIPT
Doulas' and clients' stories

Doulas' Stories

Jane Stevens

I offer live-in support as a postnatal doula, and one day not long after I'd completed my training, I received a call from a Mum who was desperately looking for immediate help. She had a three-year-old son and a month-old baby girl who suffered from severe acid reflux and colic, and when we first spoke she asked me if I was prepared to live-in for a month and work seven days a week!

I was surprised, but as I was keen to gain as much experience as possible, and I didn't have any work on at that time, after a brief chat I agreed to work six days a week for a four-week period.

I started the job four days after taking the phone call, despite the fact that I was overseas at the time. Doing live-in work has its challenges, and I live in Spain when I am not working, so on some occasions, like this one, I arrive at a job having simply chatted with the family a couple of times, and I haven't had the chance to meet them, so I've no idea what the setup is, or the standard of accommodation I will enjoy, until I arrive. By then I have a signed contract and have a deposit of one week's fee in the bank, so I can't really back out of the job, whatever surprises I find!

When I arrived, Mum opened the door and it was immediately apparent that she was exhausted. Her daughter was perched on her shoulder, her face was bright red and she was screaming her head off, and waving her arms and legs about frantically. 'She's like this most of the time she's awake', said Mum. I nearly turned on my heels and ran back to the car, but I thought that wouldn't be very professional, so I took a deep breath, and stepped over the threshold. I had only been trained to be a doula four months earlier, and I hoped that I would be up to the challenge!

The family lived in a substantial detached Georgian house set in a large, landscaped garden on the edge of a prestigious private road in a very expensive area of rural England. There was a long driveway leading up to the property, and I must confess that I felt relieved as

I saw the house, as I felt sure that I would at least have comfortable accommodation on this job, rather than a room the size of a broom cupboard, such as I'd had previously.

When I arrived, I discovered that Dad had been helping with night feeds during the first few weeks, but that he could no longer do so, as it was affecting his ability to work, so he'd recently moved into the spare bedroom and decided that I should help Mum at night in future.

Upon arrival I was told that their three-year-old son had suffered from severe acid reflux and colic until he was 15 months old, and that Mum was also lactose intolerant, and had suffered from ME in the past! It would have been good to know these things before I made the decision to take this job, and I made a mental note to ask more probing questions prior to accepting work in future. As a result of all this, fortunately Mum was being kept an eye on by both the doctor, with whom she chatted most days, and the health visitor.

I was then introduced to Nanny, who was dressed up to the nines and on her way to have her nails manicured. She was obviously relieved that I had arrived, and confirmed that baby was a sad little thing who spent much of her waking time crying and in pain. It later became apparent that she had been telling her daughter that she thought she was cuddling her baby too much, and that she should be put down and left to cry herself to sleep regularly, so that she didn't become spoiled!

I later had a chance to chat to Nanny on my own, and she told me that after her daughter's first pregnancy she had had a very tough time. She had apparently developed severe postnatal depression when she had stopped breastfeeding her son and the whole family had been affected, until Mum eventually started taking Prozac, and things settled down. As a result of the doctor's concern after her daughter arrived, there was already Prozac on the windowsill, so Mum could take it should she start to feel things were getting too much for her. She was reluctant to do so, however, as she had been told she couldn't continue to breastfeed whilst taking it, and she was very committed to doing so, and was feeding on demand, which often helped settle her daughter when little else would.

I was shown upstairs to the lovely double room where I was to stay, and there was a separate bathroom for me next door, which was a bonus. Unfortunately it was also close to their son's bedroom, which proved to be far from ideal, as I found out on the first night that he regularly woke up at night and shouted out or ran up and down the lengthy corridor crying, in search of poor Mum!

Mum and Dad doted on their two children, and had obviously lavished love and attention on their son for three years before their daughter arrived. As a result, he was remarkably bright; however, he was also rather spoilt, and was extremely jealous of his new little sister, especially when she was being breastfed. He would clamber on his Mum's lap and demand attention, and throw tantrums if his parents didn't give in to his constant demands, and after he was put to bed he would call out repeatedly for a drink, or something to eat, or ask for a story to be read to him (after he'd already heard several!), and Mum and Dad would run up and down stairs so that, even in the evenings, they had very little time to themselves.

Baby was sleeping in my room for most of the night, and since she readily took both the breast and the bottle, she generally settled down there at around 9pm, when I went upstairs with her, and she then slept until between 1am and 2am. I would wake up when baby started stirring, warm her bottle of expressed milk, change and feed her, wind her, and settle her down again until she woke up for her next feed. Sometimes this took up to an hour, but then when she woke again, between 4am and 5am, I took her into Mum to breastfeed, and then she stayed there for the rest of the night, after I had moved her Moses basket down into her room at the other end of the house and crept back to bed exhausted. Unfortunately, big brother was normally awake in the room next to mine at about 7am, and Daddy then got up to give him breakfast and get him dressed so that I could try and catch up a bit on my sleep, but I'm a light sleeper, so even though I did not have to get up at that time, I was generally woken up and couldn't get back to sleep with all that was going on around the house.

During the day, my main job was to try and comfort baby when she cried, and I'm a great fan of Dr Harvey Karp's five calming methods, which include swaddling baby. I'd been told by numerous doulas who had had much more experience than I had that this would help to calm all babies. Not this one, however! She simply fought being swaddled and just got even more upset whenever I tried it. I therefore spent many hours just wandering around the opposite end of the house from Mum, bouncing and swaying baby in my arms, singing to her, making comforting shushing sounds, and trying to ensure that she was far enough away from Mum that she couldn't be heard, as the constant sound of crying was really getting Mum down. In time, baby began to relax more, and respond to more time in someone's arms, and I also encouraged Mum to have lots of skin-to-skin contact with her, which helped calm her down.

It amuses me that so many parents look at their baby's physical characteristics and comment on the fact that their baby has their mother's nose, or their father's hair, but they never think that their baby may also have inherited Mum or Dad's personality! In this instance Mum was very confident, informed and intelligent, but she was also a rather impatient person, who, when she had decided she wanted something, wanted it immediately. Baby was just the same. She knew what she wanted, and made sure she got it in the only way she knew how, and when she was swaddled she wriggled and screamed until the blanket was removed.

Another thing I helped with was giving baby her medication, which had to be done with a syringe. Whilst I was there we tried using Infacol, Gaviscon and Colief to help with her colic, but none of these were effective and eventually she ended up being prescribed something normally only taken by adults. As the weeks went by, and things got tougher and tougher, the dose had to be increased so that, by the time I left, she was taking the maximum adult dose for it to be effective. Poor Mum was really struggling with giving her the medication, as baby needed three syringes full of it, and she hated the taste, and cried all the time it was being administered. Mum found this really distressing, and often I would hold baby while she gave it to her, and try to reassure her that she was doing the right thing. One day, not long before I left, however, she said she felt like she was 'abusing her own child' and she didn't want to continue giving her the medication. After encouraging her to chat with her mother and doctor, she decided it was time to start taking the Prozac again, which she found really difficult to do, especially as she knew it sometimes took up to six weeks before an improvement was seen.

One of the most rewarding things I did was to encourage Mum to book a haircut and a pedicure for herself, so that she had a couple of treats to look forward to. Mum booked a long appointment at the hairdressers, and I went into town with her and baby, and took baby around town in the pram while she had her hair done, which really gave her a lift. This worked really well for me too, as it is all too easy to feel 'confined to quarters' when you are in such a demanding situation. In my contract I state that I will take four hours off each day, but in reality most of this time is spent sleeping, when baby is asleep, to ensure you stay sane. I generally spent what other little time I had on the PC, keeping in touch with life in the outside world!

I also feel that I was able to help educate the grandparents a little, and help them understand just how much support their daughter needed. It seemed that Mum had brothers and sisters who all had large families and that their children were relatively easy. Nanny and Grandad therefore felt that my client was making rather a song and dance about bringing up her second child. I don't think they appreciated that this little granddaughter was not just being demanding, but was genuinely in pain a lot of the time, which was why she was crying. As time went by, they began to appreciate how hard it was for their daughter, and the level of support they offered her increased.

By the time three weeks had gone by, Mum was starting to panic about how she would manage when I left, and she decided that she would like someone else to support her for a further month when my contract ended. I helped her find someone via the internet, and suggested that it would be really useful if the next person was fully aware of the situation, and just what kind of support Mum needed, before they entered into a contract!

I learned a great deal from this job, but having done many live-in jobs now, the main thing I have learned is that every job is different, and that every mother has different ideas as to how she should bring up her baby. Our job is to support families to do what they feel is the right thing, and offer information when it is asked for, regardless of our personal feelings. Sometimes this is quite a challenge, but working with babies is wonderful, and I wouldn't change it for the world.

Supporting Attachment Parenting and Sleep by Ann Caird

This is the story of my work with an attachment parenting family as postnatal doula and then as baby sleep consultant.

I started work with R (mother) and D (father) and their first child N, who was then four weeks old, in October 2009 as a trainee postnatal doula. The purpose of my support centred on the fact that D was working away from home for several months, with only brief visits home. R required general support in the home while he was away.

I enjoyed my visits to R and N. Typically, on my arrival R and I would chat and a lovely trusting relationship developed. R was always organised with a prioritised list of things she needed help with. This was great for me as it meant I was sure of achieving what needed to be achieved, and consequently I always left R at the end of my visit with a sense of satisfaction knowing that I had provided the best practical and emotional support possible in the time we had together. Some of the tasks I helped R with included picking tomatoes, collecting prescriptions, preparing food for R, tidying clothes away and caring for N so R could take a shower... and making chocolate chip cookies for everyone! What was so special, however, was that I held N in the car while R did a quick supermarket shop – the first time R had left N for any length of time! I felt so privileged that R had trusted me with this; I knew and understood what a huge step this was for her. R and D's was a lovely attachment family – calm, nurturing and loving.

Breastfeeding was without problems and went very well, and N was so very nurtured and settled.

I completed my postnatal work with the family in January 2010. R and I kept contact; I received regular updates and photos of N's progress. R also provided me with fantastic 'verbal references' for my future clients. Not only did R talk about me as a doula, but she provided very useful information to support other mothers about what it was like to have a postnatal doula around! R has provided invaluable support and contact for my potential clients; they had the opportunity to talk to another mum about the practicalities of the postnatal doula presence in the house, and especially for one mum, the usefulness of having a prioritised list so that the family's and her own most important and pressing needs were met.

During 2010 I became a recognised doula with Doula UK, I studied and trained as an ABM peer supporter and studied for a national qualification in child sleep consultancy, with a focus on nurturing strategies rather than cry-it-out techniques. I began to take on sleep work with families with babies and children who had sleep problems alongside my doula work. R mentioned to me in September that N's sleep wasn't good, and the situation became progressively worse. Finally, in January 2011, R contacted me for help with N's sleep.

N was now not settling at all at bedtime, was waking every couple of hours throughout the night, and feeding more at night then during the day. R and D had no time for themselves – no chilling out time together, and they had both become sleep-deprived, shattered, exhausted, and frustrated with the situation.

A full investigation identified the root cause of the settling difficulties and night waking. My assessment of the situation was that 15 month old N had a 'feeding to sleep' association that had now become inappropriate for all. It was this that prevented N from settling herself to sleep and prevented her from learning how to self-soothe herself back to sleep during her natural night wakings. The only way she knew to get herself to sleep was to suckle at the breast – and this method was becoming increasingly less effective with exhausting results. N was highly dependent on R at bedtime and during the night, so D had little involvement in bedtime settling, and couldn't at that point give R a break. I knew, however, that change could be difficult for such responsive and nurturing attachment parenting parents, but I also knew that we had a good foundation for working together and making changes – our trusting, supportive and empowering doula/parent relationship. Further, I knew that R and D's nurturing and instinctive approach to parenting was the perfect foundation working with them to change N's behaviours.

Central to the sleep plan I developed for the family was D's father's role. D was to be home for two weeks, so I drew on his sensitive and instinctive approach to parenting, and also I sensed the value of empowering both parents to eventually enjoy bedtime with N, and keeping D as involved as possible despite his absences due to work. Further, R's presence would be frustrating for N at first, because unfortunately in 'feeding to sleep' issues mum equals milk, and this is what we needed to change at bedtime. D was invaluable to the success of the plan, to help and support N in developing and learning appropriate associations for sleep which were less dependent on her parents' intervention, and which in turn would support self-settling at night.

At the start of the plan, D took over the bedtime settling after the bedtime routine and earlier feed with R. D helped N to settle... it took over an hour... but once asleep she slept all night! N woke calmly and 'asked' for two early morning breastfeeds, and was so very settled! Unfortunately, though, R was so excited that she didn't sleep!

Progress continued. Using instinct and an incredible amount of patience, D gradually reduced the amount of intervention he used to settle N in her side cot. We also instigated a consistent daily routine to encourage N to take regular lunchtime naps to prevent over-tiredness and to help set her biological clock. A week into the plan, R began to help with settling, and by day ten, N had stopped asking R for milk at bedtime after her evening feed! Now R and D could take turns in settling N using a very gradual withdrawal approach.

Results??? Well, my final visit to the family was wonderful! What a difference – everyone relaxed, confident and happy! N was breastfeeding well during the day now and had greatly reduced the night feeding, everyone was getting sleep, and R and D could look forward to relaxing in the evenings. R had achieved a huge amount for her craft business as her evenings were no longer filled with the anxiety of trying to settle N... and she knew that she would be able to take evening classes to develop her skills if she wanted to. Life had turned around for the better, and the family were peaceful and happy. They had worked hard, taken time, used sensitivity and instinct, reinforced to me the invaluable support of fathers and partners, and achieved tranquillity with little crying on N's part.

The icing on the cake: I had an email recently from R, and they are pregnant again... who could wish for a happier, more positive outcome for them!

Clients' Stories

Amba Wade
Why we wanted a doula

We were expecting our baby boy at Christmas, and we had just moved to a new town where we knew very few people. We knew we were going to need some expert support in the early weeks to help us adjust and show us how to look after him. My father is a retired GP and we had arranged that he would come and stay with us for a month to give us some support. My mother died nearly fourteen years ago and if she had lived she would also have wanted to come and help us after our baby was born. My husband's mother is very elderly and the rest of his family live over a hundred miles away. What was missing from the picture was a mother figure who knew how to take care of a baby and give us both some emotional support, particularly me. Years before I had by chance picked up a leaflet about Doula UK, been interested in its work and had tucked the information away at the back of my mind.

There is a lot of help and support at the antenatal stage but very little after the baby is born and nothing that teaches you how to actually manage looking after a newborn. As my pregnancy neared its end, this gap in our knowledge was looming very large and becoming more and alarming. I remembered the information I had read about doulas and, after discussing it with my husband and father, we all agreed that booking a doula for a few weeks would help us a lot.

What attracted us to a postnatal doula?

I read through the Doula UK website and found that there were two kinds of doula, birth and postnatal. I didn't feel I needed a birth doula as I knew I would get the emotional support I needed from my husband during the birth and it would have felt intrusive. However the phrase 'mothering the mother' to describe a doula's role really resonated with all of us and we felt that a postnatal doula would be ideal for me and for the baby. After some searching via the contacts service on Doula UK we invited a local doula to come and meet us. To prepare for the meeting we used the questions suggested on the website, but we knew what would decide us would be our gut feeling and instinct.

Almost as soon as she walked through our doorway, I think we knew we had found the right doula. She had an aura of calm and knowledge and really seemed to understand our needs and our situation. We did go through the list of questions and got all the expected answers, but it was the personal connection and empathy we felt which decided us. Even in that first meeting we were very open with her because we wanted this to be the best experience it could be and get the most from it. She listened to all our concerns and gave us some excellent advice on getting ready for the birth. Although we did ask her for testimonials as a due diligence, it was a formality and we booked her very quickly, deciding on eight weeks as a starting point, with more visits at the beginning and tapering off towards the end.

How we felt about having a postnatal doula

Our postnatal doula was a godsend. The postnatal care provided by the local NHS was just not sufficient. The midwives came very rarely after the birth and were not especially helpful. The Health Visitor we had was excellent but could not have filled the gap. Without our doula I think my recovery would have been much slower and I would very probably have slipped into postnatal depression. Instead, I felt supported and cared for, which helped me to regain my emotional balance more easily. It took away some of the sting of not having my own mother with me, which I felt very strongly after the birth, especially when I saw friends who had babies at the same time as me receiving support and care from their mothers.

I had a 62-hour labour followed by an emergency caesarean section on Christmas Day. Our doula came to be with us the day after I was discharged from the hospital. At first I was emotionally and physically shattered, was very nervous about handling my baby, had no idea how to take care of his physical and emotional needs and was unsure how I felt about breastfeeding, which both he and I found difficult and traumatic. Our doula really helped us all through this major change to our lives: she was motherly and helpful, giving advice, taking care of the baby for the four hours she was with us, showing us how to take care of him and being a very reassuring and calming presence. She got on well with all of us, connecting with my father and my mother-in-law who had also come to stay for a few days.

She took care of the whole family by cooking delicious lunches and helping with housework and ironing, which made a huge difference to us. She spent a lot of time with me, talking, reassuring, encouraging, making sure that I rested and ate properly and helping me to bond even more closely with my baby. As I recovered and became more active, she listened to my fears and helped me to build up my confidence by taking the baby out in his pram for walks and shopping trips and showing me how to entertain him, communicate with him and play with him.

She understood what was important to me and each time she came I could see evidence of her thoughtfulness and empathy in how she took care of the house and family. I was able to really open up to her and tell her how I was feeling – this is difficult for me as I am a fairly private person, but she made it easy. Being this open also helped me to cope and recover more quickly.

After about two months we began to wind down and the nature of the relationship changed a little according to what I needed. I was more in control, formed my own strong views about my baby's care, understood his needs much more and had bonded with him very strongly. I called on her knowledge of baby behaviour to help me understand what he was telling me and to help me set his routine. By this time our doula was coming just once a week rather than two or three times a week and though we extended her booking for another month to continue the support and advice we had come to rely on, she and I felt I was ready to fly on my own.

Going forward

Our postnatal doula showed me how to be a mother. I think that is the most meaningful testimonial. While we have completed our formal time together, we haven't completely ended the relationship. We have asked our doula to come back for one-off occasions and as we hope to have another baby soon we have also asked her to come back then to take care of us once more.

Sonia
My experience of having a postnatal doula

I felt extremely privileged to be able have Naomi as my postnatal doula, and in some ways came to think of her as my 'hire a mum'. Naomi was recommended by a friend and in fact worked with several of our social group. Naomi arrived when our first baby was just under two weeks old and helped us to make sense of the lovely chaos that had become our world. As a new mum, she guided me with how to look after my newborn. Everything from sleep and feeding routine to play time and development activities. Simple things like nappy off and tummy time, using the play-gym.

In addition, being sent to bed for a sleep to wake up with a happy baby being brought to me along with a cup of tea and toast and the delicious smells of dinner wafting up from the kitchen, and then to find the washing done, made a huge difference. Naomi stayed with us until our baby was three months old, when I very reluctantly had to admit that it was time for her to move on!

When I became pregnant two months later (intentionally!), it was without a moment's hesitation that we contacted Naomi and asked for her help. In fact, I couldn't have imagined her not being there! This time it was a very different family dynamic, introducing a fourteen-month-old to her newborn baby sister. There was a lot of confusion, frustration and anger from her that she could no longer have her mummy as and when she needed me. Add to this the very different, competing needs of a breastfeeding newborn (plus a hormonal mum) and you have quite a highly emotion situation. Naomi was calm, neutral and normalised the whole thing. There were times that I found Naomi in many ways as a role model for parenting (e.g. involving my fourteen-month-old in cleaning/caring tasks, something I would never have thought of, yet so obvious). My fourteen-month-old observed everything and had clearly watched Naomi bring me a cushion when breastfeeding, and started to do this unprompted herself. Naomi encouraged me to find balance, time for everyone and came up with practical strategies to help with all of this.

Nutrition was an area Naomi helped me to focus on, which I would have otherwise ignored. Breast milk needs food and water, and sleep deprivation needs dietary support or you can become quite run down. Naomi helped me to understand this, and provided delicious meals and snacks as an incentive. She is an awesome cook!

Naomi is very talented at what she does, I never felt pressured to do anything, in fact often didn't realise that I was 'doing' what had been very subtly suggested, thinking it was my idea! It was only on reflection after Naomi left that I realised I was doing these things! I never felt judged, criticised or 'told', quite the opposite. Warm, genuine, affection, regard and support (despite my sleep-deprived ramblings). It was a joy to share special family moments with her, e.g. my fourteen-month-old's first steps. Naomi was there at the end of the phone at the most fraught moments, always calm and supportive. As a result, we felt we had a 'guide' through a very special, wonderful yet challenging and life-changing time. It helped us both to gain in confidence.

RECIPES

Providing tasty snacks and meals will be a huge boost for a new mother. She may not have time, or even remember, to feed herself as she tends to her baby. Of course what you can produce will be dictated by what is available. Even if a kitchen appears to have very little in, it is surprising what you can rustle up! (See below, 'Nothing in the cupboard' soup.) You don't have to be a gourmet cook, just know how to prepare a few easy, nourishing dishes. It is amazing how food, lovingly prepared and presented, can provide such a well-needed comfort and source of renewed energy.

A word about ingredients and equipment

The only piece of kitchen gadgetry that I would struggle to do without is a hand-held blender. As with baby equipment I would never push people to buy unnecessary things. However, if your friend/daughter/client does not have one, they are invaluable not only for food preparation (smoothies, soups, dips), but also later on for weaning.

I always cook more than necessary for just one meal. I make larger quantities so that there is always enough for a further few meals, or pack them for freezing and future use.

Good store-cupboard ingredients

This is the time to encourage nutritionally dense foods. This list can be suggested to parents before you arrive.

> *Full-fat* milk and yoghurt will provide a more nutritious component to recipes. The essential calcium, vitamins and minerals are present in abundance compared to the low-fat equivalent. This is *not* the time for low-fat or calorie counting.

> Tahini – creamed sesame seeds. High in protein and more calcium than milk, available from health food shops, Middle Eastern and Asian stores and some supermarkets. Excellent drizzled on savoury dishes and to make humous.

> Quinoa – one cup of cooked quinoa (185g) contains 8.14 grams of protein.

> Wholemeal pasta.

> Brown rice.

> Rolled oats.

> Soy sauce – avoid the small, expensive soy sauce containing sugar. Buy large bottles from any health food store.

> Mixed nuts – expensive when bought in small quantities from supermarkets. Instead purchase from a health food store, where they are often on offer.

> Dried fruits: apricots, figs, prunes, raisins and so on.

> Nut butters – almond butter and cashew nut butter are delicious and highly nutritious, particularly if avoiding peanuts. Great on oatcakes for a between-meals blood sugar boost.

> Fruit spreads – sugar free.

Smoothie

Equal quantities of milk and full-fat live natural yoghurt
Banana
Blueberries and/or raspberries, strawberries, mango (fresh or frozen)
1 tbsp ground almonds
2 tsp honey
1 tsp vanilla extract (optional)

Place all ingredients in large jug. Blend well. Store covered in the fridge. Will be fine for 24 hours.

Mixed nuts and seeds snack

Any combination of mixed nuts: brazils, cashews, hazelnuts, walnuts, almonds
Seeds: pumpkin and/or sunflower

Place nuts in a large non-stick frying pan on stove. Dry roast in the pan until they start to brown, then add seeds. Keep a close eye so they don't burn, turning regularly. Once all evenly browned, after approximately ten minutes, turn off heat. Add a good splash of soy sauce and a tablespoon of honey or agave syrup.

These are delicious as they are but can be made slightly spicy. Add 1 tsp of cumin powder and 1 tsp of garlic powder, or 1 tsp curry powder.

Stir well and leave to cool. Once cool add (optional) dried chopped dates, apricots, cranberries and/or raisins.

Store in an airtight container. I usually pack two small tubs, one for the bedside and one for snacking in the living area.

Easy, no-peel roasted vegetable soup

Any medium-sized pumpkin or squash
Sweet potatoes or carrots
4 onions
Vegetable or chicken stock
Tin of coconut milk
1 tsp curry paste, or 2 tsp each ground cumin and ground coriander

Cut all vegetables in half. Place skin side up on lightly oiled baking tray. Roast approx. 45 minutes, until soft.

Simmer the stock, coconut milk and spices for 10 minutes while vegetables are roasting.

Scoop out seeds from pumpkin. Lift the skins off the onions and discard. Then scoop out flesh and add with all the other veg into liquid. Blend. Garnish with fresh coriander and parsley.

∞∞∞∞∞∞∞∞∞ Butternut squash soup ∞∞∞∞∞∞∞∞∞

2 medium butternut squash or 1 large squash or pumpkin
4 onions
Tin of coconut milk
Curry paste
Vegetable cube or bouillon
Water

Split the squash and onions and lay skin side up on an oiled baking tray. Roast approx 40 minutes until soft. Meanwhile simmer the coconut milk, spices and stock.
Once cooked scoop out and discard seeds. Remove onion skins. Add all to stock. Simmer further 10 minutes. Leave to cool for 10 mins then liquidise. Garnish with plenty of chopped fresh coriander.

∞∞∞∞∞∞∞∞∞ Chicken soup ∞∞∞∞∞∞∞∞∞

This soup is renowned across many cultures for its nourishing properties.

1 whole chicken
3 stalks celery with leaves, chopped
1 pound carrots
2 onions, chopped
2 stock cubes: beef, vegetable, or chicken
1 tsp mixed dry herbs
5 black peppercorns
2 bay leaves

Place chicken in a large pot and cover with water. Place celery leaves in pot and bring to a boil, then reduce heat and simmer until chicken is cooked through, 30 to 40 minutes. Remove chicken from pot and place in a bowl until cool enough to handle.
Meanwhile, strain the cooking liquid, discard the celery tops and place the cooking liquid in a large pot. Place celery, carrots, onion, bouillon, and chicken broth in the pot and let simmer. Season with thyme, poultry seasoning, basil, peppercorns, bay leaves and parsley.
Bone chicken and cut up meat into bite-size pieces. Return meat to

pot. Cook until vegetables are tender and flavours are well blended, up to 90 minutes.

Optional: 10 minutes before serving add any pasta or noodles.

Brown rice/vegetable tahini dish

Cook brown rice.

Sauté onion, garlic and fresh ginger. Add grated carrot... till nearly done. Then add frozen peas. Mix with rice. Drizzle with tahini, soy sauce and lemon juice and season with black pepper.

Good hot or cold.

'Nothing in the cupboard' soup

Onions, potatoes, carrots

Frozen peas, sweetcorn, any vegetable

Tins tomatoes, pulses

Marmite, stock cubes

Sauté chopped onions and carrots till half cooked. Add water with spoonful of marmite, tin of tomatoes. Simmer 10 minutes, then add fresh or frozen vegetables. Serve with grated cheese (if available) and bread.

'Whole' meal salad

Cook and leave to cool: wholewheat pasta, quinoa, couscous or brown rice.

Add the following:

Chopped cucumber, carrots, peppers, radish, tomato, celery, spring or red onion, sundried tomato

Sunflower seeds, pumpkin seeds, any chopped nuts

Chopped feta (optional)

Dress with plenty of lemon juice, soy sauce and drizzle with tahini and a swirl of live natural yoghurt.

∞∞∞∞∞∞∞∞∞∞ **Pasta salad** ∞∞∞∞∞∞∞∞∞∞

Cook pasta.
Make dressing in a large bowl. Equal quantities of mayonnaise and yoghurt, a tablespoon of grainy mustard and the juice of half a lemon. Add chopped salad ingredients as above and a tin of drained tuna (optional). Mix well.

∞∞∞∞∞∞∞∞∞∞ **Flapjacks** ∞∞∞∞∞∞∞∞∞∞

6 oz butter
4 tbsp honey, syrup, brown sugar
1 tsp black treacle or molasses
8 oz rolled oats
1 tbsp sesame seeds, desiccated coconut, flaked or ground almonds
Few drops vanilla extract
Pinch of salt

Melt butter and syrups. Add to dry ingredients. Mix well. Press firmly into greased flat baking tray. Bake 15 mins until golden brown. For an extra special treat, make chocolate flapjacks – once they are cooked turn off the oven, leave tray in oven and place plain chocolate squares evenly over the top and spread once melted. Remove from oven to cool.

∞∞∞∞∞∞∞∞∞∞ **Carrot Cake** ∞∞∞∞∞∞∞∞∞∞

6 oz light brown or muscovado sugar
6 fl oz sunflower oil
3 eggs, lightly beaten
4 medium carrots, grated
4 oz raisins
Grated rind of large orange and/or lemon
6 oz self-raising wholemeal or white flour
1 tsp bicarbonate of soda
1 tsp cinammon
1/2 tsp grated or ground nutmeg

Preheat oven to 180°C/GM 4. Grease and line square cake tin.

Lightly mix sugar, oil and eggs in large bowl. Stir in carrots, raisins and rind.

Sift dry ingredients into the bowl. Mix lightly until mixture is soft and runny.

Pour mixture into the tin and bake approx. 45 minutes. Cool in tin for 5 minutes before turning out, removing greaseproof paper and cooling on a wire rack.

Icing (Optional. Perfectly nice with or without!)

30 g butter, room temperature

60 g cream cheese

1/2 tsp vanilla extract

3/4 cup sieved icing sugar

Cream the butter, cream cheese and vanilla extract until smooth. Gradually mix in the icing sugar and beat until smooth. Allow cake to completely cool before spreading with icing.

Oatmeal Cookies

1 cup raisins

1 cup butter, melted

1 tsp vanilla extract

3 eggs (large)

1 cup dark brown sugar

1 cup granulated sugar

2.5 cups self-raising flour

1 tsp cinnamon

2 tsp baking powder

1 1/2 cups rolled oats

1/2 cup wheatgerm

3/4 cup pecans or walnuts

1 cup chocolate chips (optional)

Preheat oven to 180°C. In a bowl soak the raisins in the melted butter and vanilla for an hour. Add the eggs and sugar and beat well. In a separate bowl, combine flour, salt, cinnamon, baking powder, oats and wheatgerm. Slowly add the dry mixture to the wet. Stir in the pecans, walnuts and chocolate chips by hand if using. Spoon on to greased baking sheets. Bake for 10 to 15 mins.

Granola

125g butter/ sunflower or grape seed oil
150ml honey
1 tbsp black treacle
1 tsp vanilla
500g oat flakes
100g desiccated coconut
100g flaked almonds
100g any nuts available (brazils, cashews etc)
100g pumpkin seeds
100g sunflower seeds
200–300g mixed dried fruit (chopped apricots, dates, figs, raisins, sultanas, dried blueberries, cranberries, goji berries, dried cherries etc)

Preheat the oven to 160°C/Fan 140°C/GM 3. Place butter and honey, treacle and oil in a small pan on a low heat to melt.

Mix remaining ingredients except dried fruit in a large bowl. Mix in butter and honey mix, stir well. Spread out in large tin and toast in the oven for about 25 mins until golden. Stir about every five minutes to keep the toasting even and stop the outside burning.

Leave to cool. Once cooled, stir in the dried fruit and store in an airtight container.

Delicious with milk or sprinkled over natural yoghurt.

Apple/pear/plum and/or blackberry crumble

8 oz oats
4 oz butter
2 oz ground almonds
1 tsp cinnamon and or ginger
6 oz dark brown sugar

Chop apples, blackberries, plums, handful raisins and/or dried apricots (optional)

Just cover with water and place in large ovenproof dish.

Rub butter into dry ingredients until crumbly appearance. Add sugar. Sprinkle over the fruit. Gently tamp down. Bake in medium oven for approx 45 minutes until golden brown on top.

Vegetable tray bake

Chop to similar size chunks all or any of the following: potatoes, sweet potatoes, squash, celeriac, carrots, parsnips and onions, skinned and quartered.

On a large baking dish pour some mild olive oil/vegetable oil. Ensure the whole area is covered. Next pour in the vegetables, mixing and coating with a little more oil.

Bake at 150°C for approx 30 minutes. Then mix thoroughly, sprinkle with salt and black pepper, rosemary and/or oregano. Crisp up for a further 10 minutes.

Remove from oven. Drizzle with a little balsamic vinegar and serve as an accompaniment to a main course, or as it is with grated cheese.

Groaning Cake

(by Jess Booth, doula)

A groaning cake is a rich, spiced cake that traditionally women bake during labour (hence the name). The ingredients are flexible and it is a completely forgiving recipe so feel free to experiment by adding pumpkin, banana or berries, for example.

3 cups flour (I use a combination of spelt and einkorn flour)
2 tsp baking powder
1 tsp baking soda
1 tbsp cinnamon
1/2 tsp cloves
1 tbsp fresh ginger
1/2 sweet potato peeled and grated
1 big apple grated
1 carrot grated
1/2 cup walnuts or pecans, chopped
1/2 cup chopped dates and apricots
1/4 cup orange juice
4 eggs
1/4 cup blackstrap molasses
1 tsp almond extract

1 cup honey
3/4 cup coconut oil – melted

Heat the oven to 180°C and grease and line bottom of pans with baking parchment (I usually fill four 1/2 lb loaf pans).

Soak the dried fruit in 1/4 cup of orange juice.

In a bowl mix together flour, baking powder, baking soda, cinnamon and cloves.

In another bowl lightly beat eggs, and add the rest of the ingredients to the eggs including the dates and apricots in the orange juice.

Add the wet to the dry and mix until just combined.

Divide mixture into four loaf tins and bake for about 40 minutes or until a skewer inserted in middle comes out clean.

Allow to cool. This tastes great served warm with butter or a dollop of cream. It can also be eaten cold. The extras freeze well.

Energy Balls

2 cups cashews, almonds or walnuts or any combination
1 cup unsweetened dessicated coconut
2 cups soft pitted dates
1 teaspoon vanilla extract
1/2 teaspoon salt
2 tablespoons coconut oil

Blend all the above in a food processor. Shape into small balls and place in freezer for an hour to set. Can be rolled in dessicated coconut and/or cocoa powder for a fancier finish. Remove to fridge where they will keep for a week.

USEFUL CONTACTS

Always check first the hours that the phones are manned, as they are mostly operated by volunteers.

BREASTFEEDING
Association of Breastfeeding Mothers
0300 3305453   abm.me.uk
La Leche League 0845 120 2918 laleche.org.uk
National Childbirth Trust 0300 330 0700 nct.org.uk
National Breastfeeding Helpline 0300 100 0212
Breastfeeding Network 0300 100 0210
breastfeedingnetwork.org.uk
Lactation Consultants of Great Britain lcgb.org
ATP – Association of Tongue-Tie Practitioners tongue-tie.org.uk
UKAMB – United Kingdom Association for Milk Banking ukamb.org

BIRTH TRAUMA
The Birth Trauma Association
birthtraumaassociation.org.uk

POSTNATAL DEPRESSION
The Association For Postnatal Illness
020 7386 0868 apni.org
Pandas – Pre and Postnatal Depression Advice and Support 0843 2898401 pandasfoundation.org.uk
Mind mind.org.uk 03001233393
Samaritans 08457 909090 (24 hours) samaritans.org

PARENTS SUPPORT
Mumsnet mumsnet.com
National Childbirth Trust nct.org.uk

CRYING BABY
Cry-sis 08451 228 669 www.cry-sis.org.uk

BEREAVEMENT
Child Bereavement UK 08000288840
childbereavement.org.uk
The Lullaby Trust (formerly Foundation for the Study of
Infant deaths) 0808 802 6868 lullabytrustinmemory.org.uk
Miscarriage Association 01924 200 799
miscarriageassociation.org.uk
Stillbirth and Neonatal Death Society 020 7436 5881
uk-sands.org
The Compassionate Friends (UK) 0845 123 2304
tcf.org.uk
The Child Death Helpline 0800 282 986
childdeathhelpline.org.uk

PARENTS OF CHILDREN WITH SPECIAL NEEDS
Contact a Family 0808 808 3555 cafamily.org.uk

PARENTS WITH MULTIPLES
Twin and Multiple Birth Association 0800 138 0509
tamba.org.uk
The Multiple Births Foundation 020 3313 3519
multiplebirths.org.uk

GRANDPARENTS
The Grandparents' Association 0845 4349585
grandparents-association.org.uk

RELATIONSHIP SUPPORT
Relate 0300 100 1234 relate.org.uk

DOULAS
Doula UK (find a doula/doula training) doula.org.uk

APPENDIX 1

Questions to ask a Prospective Postnatal Doula

When making initial telephone contact:

Date
Name of doula
Doula's email address
Doula's telephone number

1. Are you available around my due date?
2. How long have you been a doula, how many families have you been a doula for?
3. What doula certification do you have or what courses have you attended?
4. How much do you charge, and what is included? Is there a deposit to pay?
5. Do you draw up a written contract? Can I see a copy?
6. Do you have a backup? Who is your backup, and can I meet her? Under what circumstances would you send your backup?
7. How many hours a day are you available, and do you have a minimum number of hours?
8. Do you do nights (is the hourly rate different)?
9. Do we have to pay your travel costs in addition to the hourly rate?
10. What happens if, for personal reasons, you are unable to be our postnatal doula after the birth and your backup is also unavailable? Will our deposit be fully refunded?
11. What happens if we decide nearer to, or after, the birth that we no longer require a postnatal doula? What monies will be due to you?

During a face-to-face interview:

1. What part of your job do you enjoy most?
2. What skills and abilities do you personally feel you bring to your doula role?
3. What is your philosophy of childbirth and your work as a doula?

4. What books do you recommend to new parents?
5. How do you handle conflicts with family members or medical professionals?
6. How would you address this issue I have? (If you have a particular concern about the birth or postnatal period e.g. physical, emotional or psychological.)
7. Can you provide references?
8. Do you have children?
9. How is your childcare organised (what would happen if your child was sick when it is planned that you come to work for me?)
10. What is your availability? What other doula jobs have you got booked around the dates that I may need you? For example, could you stay a few extra hours at the last minute (emergency or if mother is unwell)?
11. Are you insured?
12. Have you had a police check?
13. Do you have a valid driving licence?
14. Do you know first aid?
15. How do you feel about breastfeeding and what is your experience of it?
16. What if I have a breastfeeding/bottle feeding problem? What can you do to help me?
17. How would you describe your philosophies on parenting?
18. Can we telephone/email you before the birth with postnatal questions/concerns we have been thinking about?
19. How do you view housework? What are you prepared to do?

As a parent you may want to think about the following points when thinking about employing a postnatal doula:

1. Does she listen to me well?
2. Will she respect my wishes?
3. Will my partner/children like her?
4. Do I want to spend day after day with this postnatal doula?

Doula UK

APPENDIX 2

Infant Feeding Guidance Paper for Doula UK

by Maddie McMahon based on the UNICEF BFI 7 steps to breastfeeding support in the community

Introduction

The template used for this paper is the World Health Organisation and UNICEF Baby Friendly Seven Point Plan for the promotion, protection and support of Breastfeeding in Community health care settings. It takes into account the particular circumstances of doulas working as members of Doula UK, which endorses and aligns itself strongly with the Baby Friendly Initiative.

The Baby Friendly Initiative is a worldwide programme launched in 1992, to encourage maternity hospitals to implement the Ten Steps to Successful Breastfeeding and to practise in accordance with the International Code of Marketing of Breastmilk Substitutes. The BFI came to the UK in 1994 and, in 1998, its principles were extended to cover the work of community healthcare services in the Seven Point Plan.

UK breastfeeding rates over the succeeding 10 years indicate that, while there have been significant increases in breastfeeding initiation, early discontinuation rates remain unacceptably high.

Doula UK is aware that breastfed babies have less chance of diarrhoea and vomiting and having to go to hospital as a result; have fewer chest and ear infections, less likelihood of developing Type 2 diabetes and less chance of developing eczema.

The NHS also recommends breastfeeding as being good for mothers as it lowers the risk of getting breast and ovarian cancer in later life and can help build a strong bond between mother and baby.

Doula UK believes their doulas are ideally placed to have an impact not only on initiation rates, but also on duration of breastfeeding. Recent surveys have concluded that the majority of women report their breastfeeding relationships ceased before they were happy to stop. Doulas have a key part to play in supporting women with information, signposting and practical help to begin and to continue breastfeeding for as long as they wish.

Our Approach to Training

In order for doulas to have the knowledge to support their clients unconditionally, DUK believes it is essential to provide equal opportunities for learning, so all our practitioners have a basic understanding of normal breastfeeding management.

DUK aims to provide a supportive atmosphere to enable doulas to debrief from their own infant-feeding experiences and to encourage them to work in the spirit of Baby Friendly and the WHO Code on the Marketing of Breastmilk Substitutes: ('The aim of this Code is to contribute to the provision of safe and adequate nutrition for infants, by the protection and promotion of breastfeeding, and by ensuring the proper use of breastmilk substitutes, when these are necessary, on the basis of adequate information and through appropriate marketing and distribution.')

It is also our view that just as a doula makes a commitment to normal birth (whilst remaining unswerving in her unconditional support for women who choose, or find themselves experiencing, a medicalised birth), she should also undertake a commitment to supporting breastfeeding – whilst remaining supportive of those clients who choose, or end up, artificially feeding.

Point 1 – Initial Doula Preparation Courses

DUK aims to provide all new doulas with basic infant feeding knowledge and skills during their initial doula preparation course, including knowledge of the WHO Code and the Unicef Baby Friendly Initiative.

> All doulas supporting breastfeeding mothers and babies or mothers who are making infant-feeding choices, are to be up to date on basic breastfeeding management.

> All doulas are to be aware of their boundaries and the scope of their knowledge and be able to signpost to more specialist support where necessary.

Point 2 – Doulas will endeavour to inform all pregnant women about the benefits and management of normal breastfeeding

All pregnant women should receive full and clear information about the health benefits of breastfeeding and the importance of/ relevance of:

> skin contact after delivery
> posture, positioning, approach and attachment
> sleeping in the same room as their baby and rooming-in in hospital (or bedsharing, should the mother choose this)
> baby-led feeding (on demand)
> avoiding supplements, teats and dummies

All written materials intended for pregnant women should be accurate and effective, and free from the promotion of breastmilk substitutes, bottles, teats and dummies.

Pregnant women should not be given instruction on how to prepare bottles of infant formula as part of antenatal sessions, but doulas are to have a clear knowledge of up-to-date DH guidelines on making up powdered infant milk to pass on to clients who have chosen to formula feed or who need to for medical reasons.

Point 3 – Support mothers to initiate and maintain breastfeeding

DUK doulas will have a basic understanding of how breastfeeding works and be able to:

> see signs in the baby that indicate sufficient milk intake: urine output, stooling, general condition of the baby including weight-gain and length (eg going up to next size nappies/sleepsuit)
> see signs in the mother that indicate effective feeding: comfortable breasts, no evidence of nipple pain or damage.
> recognise effective milk transfer and where to refer for help if needed.
> explain feeding and how to recognise feeding cues
> suggest strategies for coping with night-time feeds
> provide basic information on expressing (hand and pump) and be knowledgeable about its potential importance in the prevention and management of breastfeeding challenges such as engorgement and mastitis.
> offer breastfeeding mothers information on how they can continue to breastfeed if and when they return to work.
> have basic knowledge of how to support and encourage mothers in positioning their babies and latching them on effectively, without pain – and signpost knowledge should this prove difficult.

Point 4 – Encourage exclusive and continued breastfeeding, with appropriately timed introduction of complementary foods

> All breastfeeding mothers will be encouraged by DUK doulas to breastfeed exclusively for around six months, and have the reasons for this recommendation explained to them.

> They will be informed about the appropriate age for introducing complementary foods and drinks, alongside breastmilk.

> Doulas will be able to answer basic questions on the many benefits of breastfeeding both to babies and mothers.

> DUK doulas will not promote or recommend infant food or drink other than breastmilk, nor signpost to particular brands.

> Doulas will have a basic understanding of the WHO Code and work within its scope and spirit.

Point 5 – Protecting the space for breastfeeding

All breastfeeding mothers should be given the opportunity to discuss their feelings about feeding in public places, and given tips for doing so discreetly should this be appropriate for her. The doula can provide mothers with information about places locally where breastfeeding is known to be welcomed.

Point 6 – Promote co-operation between doulas, healthcare staff, breastfeeding support groups and local community

> All breastfeeding mothers should be informed which health professional(s) to contact for breastfeeding support and how to access this help (eg counsellors or support groups).

> Women should be informed about how they can access help with breastfeeding outside office hours (NB: this does not need to cover 24 hours).

Point 7 – Mothers who are formula feeding

The needs of these mothers will not be overlooked by DUK doulas.

Many of the criteria for the care of breastfeeding mothers and babies are equally applicable to mothers and babies who are formula feeding, while others have matching equivalents that would be considered good practice. Doulas will be able to provide:

> appropriate signposting to up-to-date guidance on making up

powdered formula

> information about the benefits of babies being kept near their parents

> information to enable safe night-time care for all babies

> information about how to recognise feeding cues and ensure babies are fed at appropriate intervals

> information about the appropriate age for introducing complementary foods

Particular care and planning is needed to ensure that mothers who begin breastfeeding but who later wish to change to formula feeding are given full support and are provided with appropriate and timely additional information about formula feeding (or how to combine breastfeeding with the use of formula).

APPENDIX 3

My experiences at Naxal Orphanage, Kathmandu, supported by the charity OCCED

I planned to work in the orphanage for a month and hoped to contribute my time, experience and energy to a worthy cause. It was hard to envisage this unknown life and what my time there would entail. As I had seen some pictures of the orphanage before my visit I already had some idea of the conditions to expect. As I approached it I was impressed by the smart exterior. It is a solid brick building with a very impressive gold OCCED sign. As I was shown around the back it was a completely different story. The building was quite derelict in areas and badly dilapidated in places. I understand that funds are being collected and the search is on for new, larger premises.

My experience of caring for babies in the UK had been in immaculately clean maternity units or in clean, well-equipped homes. Before arriving in Nepal I had imagined that I would be put in a situation where the institution was perhaps not coping so well. I pictured myself being given responsibility for 'lots' of small, newly-orphaned babies. The reality was very different... There were forty-three children. The youngest infant was nine months old, in a group of ten toddlers up to about the age of two. Many children arrive there when they are only a few weeks old; mothers commonly die in childbirth or babies are unwanted or illegitimate and therefore rejected. There are two 'didis' (women who care, as mothers, for the orphans) in charge of the ten little ones: they are with them twenty-four hours a day and have full responsibility for their needs. There is a resident nurse and a doctor checks them weekly. My initial reaction was 'What can I do here?' Everyone was so capable and coping admirably. So for the first few days I observed their routine and tried to find ways that I could 'help'

or lessen their load. I saw how they washed the children with wet cotton wool, never bathed them, and then massaged them all over, very vigorously, with mustard oil. The babies appeared to really enjoy this firm touch compared to the very light massage performed on our babies in the West – I imagine it made them feel secure. At first I felt uncomfortable as my way was so different and I saw the 'didis' giggling at my delicate touch. So I decided to follow their method, realising that it was an effective technique which the babies responded to enthusiastically.

In my 'work' with babies I always instinctively give my all: cuddling, hugging, calming and settling. This experience was immediately challenged when it was explained to me that the didis prefer that volunteers don't favour one child. The children can very quickly become attached and then, when the volunteer leaves, the babies are more demanding and unsettled. So I soon learnt to 'unpeel' them from me and share my attention around. Once the children got to know me they would 'bomb' me as soon as I entered the nursery! This was really unsettling, but I discovered that if I brought with me something new and distracting, like a basket of bricks borrowed from the older kids, they would play very happily.

It is traditional and quite normal to use cut-up cotton fabric for nappies unless you are wealthy and can afford disposables. The orphanage used old sheets and even old clothes cut into squares. These were tied with a knot and the baby was then dressed. No pins or plastic pants were used. They used no wet wipes, cleansers or creams ever… compare this to our over-sanitised use of products! I never once saw a case of nappy rash. However, the babies were wet through very quickly and needed changing continuously, which created mountains of laundry. As a result of the poor nappy situation I often got soaked and was often stepping in pee on the floor! I was very intent on achieving a mission of change by introducing, at the very least, thicker fabric.

Another *very* noticeable difference was the early introduction to potty training. Every morning the children were placed on a potty and left there until they performed. I was totally amazed to only see two poos in nappies in four weeks!

Although I believe it is good to encourage babies to play alone, they do need a certain amount of stimulation. The didis are often too exhausted or busy to play with the children. I found they loved the extra singing, playing and clapping I could offer, which encouraged them to be more active.

In the mornings the babies would play on the roof area. To get there they had to negotiate dangerous chipped steps, open banisters and uneven ground. Some of them were only barely walking, but they were all so careful and, given this opportunity, had learnt to be sure-footed. On arriving at the roof area they would constantly be leaning over and trying to climb the low wall. I was initially shocked and wondered why they didn't make it safer. When I suggested this [through a translator] they were shocked and asked 'Why?' – they were there to constantly watch over them. I felt a bit bad, as if I had insulted their responsibility. This exchange highlighted for me our health and safety paranoia in the West. Another observation I made was that the children had nothing to play with compared to the abundance of toys provided to most children in the West, who are over-stimulated with so many mechanical and electronic toys, vibrating chairs and so on. Again my immediate thought was 'These children need some toys'. But I kept quiet and immediately saw how they played happily together like a pack of cubs, tumbling, chasing, finding specks of dust to amuse them.

When children did fall on the hard concrete floor, they nearly always picked themselves up and carried on. This was another example of how the didis would only intervene if a baby was clearly in danger. If they were fighting over a toy they were left to sort it out themselves and I was amazed to see them actually swapping toys!

I have total respect and admiration for OCCED, the charity that runs this orphanage. I *know* that these children are the lucky ones. They are alive, healthy, thriving and most importantly loved, compared to the many many little ones out on the street.

I really hope that I did make a difference and introduced some positive practical changes. With the generous donations from friends and family I bought:

> A big supply of baby bottles, so they had one each. I was shocked to see them having to share and take turns with only four bottles. They were always screaming. When I left they were all happy and settled with their own bottle at nap time.

> A training beaker each, which by the time I left they were all using very well.

> New knives, buckets, bowls, bins, cooking utensils, glasses and so on to completely re-equip the sparse and frugal kitchen.

> Thirty meters of Thomas the Tank Engine cotton to make new bed sheets.

> Contributed to the coach cost and extra snacks for an outing for all the children to a botanical garden, where they played joyfully on grass, skipped, played and had a picnic. This was a rare treat as, apart from the older ones going to school, the children rarely leave the orphanage.

> Some towels, which the didis were delighted to discover were thick enough to use as nappies.

> The practical tips I introduced included:

> Teaching babies to drink from trainer cups. This also meant that they now have water twice in the day instead of only at nap times.

> Fruit once a day, instead of sweet biscuits twice.

> Putting the children on the potty more often.

> Introducing more stimulating toys each day.

More things I did to lighten the load for the didis: folded cloths for nappies, folded laundry, washed cups, bottles and so on, kept an eye when they left the nursery, got babies ready and up from sleep. I also compiled some helpful guidelines for new volunteers to read before they start.

Other experiences

Despite being at the orphanage every day I managed to have a huge variety of other memorable experiences. I chose to stay with a Nepalese family, rather than in a hotel, which I know enriched my experience enormously. I ate their food, tolerated the Nepalese-style toilet and shared their lifestyle, culture, religion and yoga. I was invited to a wedding, to a traditional dance performance, and got taken to the best local shopping markets. Thanks to Social Tours I was shown many sights and went on a trek with my own personal guide. I also witnessed one of the largest Hindu festivals, and lots more...

I was also very honoured to be invited by the presidents of the charity to travel to three remote areas where their charity is running a literacy project for women. I was a guest speaker and was overwhelmed by their commitment and determination. I also trekked three hours to a remote community where OCCED were providing an eye clinic. They invite all local people in the surrounding area to be screened for cataracts. Those diagnosed are then provided with transport to the eye hospital in Kathmandu, where they have the operation (no charge). It is an incredible, life-changing opportunity for these people. The Nepalese are the most kind, generous and loving people I have ever encountered. I had the most wonderful and rewarding time and was showered with gifts, garlands and thanks on my departure. Although I tried not to get too emotionally attached to the babies, I still wept when I left.

APPENDIX 4

Supporting visually impaired parents
by Gemma Edwards

Here are some of the things I believe it is helpful for supportive people to bear in mind, with regard to VI parents in those early days.

Support, don't take over!
When spending time with a tired and anxious new parent, it's tempting to leap in and give them a break, taking over practical tasks yourself. Whilst I doubt many new parents would object to having one less dirty nappy to change in a day, as a general rule, it will boost a VI parent's confidence more if you can support them to do things for themselves. As new parents, we can easily fall into feeling self-conscious and judged, and this is particularly so for those of us who are VI. We may worry that we are not coming up to other people's standards of 'good' parenting, especially if others are keen to do things for us at every opportunity. This insecurity can be compounded when we see sighted friends or relatives doing basic tasks like nappy changing and making up feeds quicker than we can ourselves. Remember that it is important to all mums' self-confidence to feel they are competent to feed and look after their babies. Also bear in mind that, particularly in the early weeks, the daily routines of washing and changing are likely to take a little longer for a VI parent, but that this isn't a problem in itself. After all, the baby won't mind if nappy changes or walks to the shops take twice as long now as they will in three months' time!

There's more than one way to do nearly everything!
If someone you know is a VI parent-to-be, it can be difficult to imagine how they will manage to do all the tasks you are so used to doing with full sight. However, most VI parents will manage to carry out the daily routines of babycare, given some practice and with some adjustments to suit themselves. Remember that most VI people have already developed a range of skills for coping with ordinary daily activities, before becoming parents. Those of us who have had time to adjust to sight loss, or who have always been VI, will be able to carry out tasks quite easily which would confound

most sighted people if suddenly blind-folded and set the challenge! So try not to get too bogged down in picturing how you personally would do things in their position.

When we imagine doing something like going out for a walk with a baby, we imagine doing it the way we personally do it. For a sighted parent, that is likely to mean walking down the street pushing a buggy. For a VI parent, going for a walk may involve carrying their baby in a sling, or pulling a buggy behind them while they use a white cane or work a guidedog.

There are many daily tasks which VI parents do slightly, or very, differently from sighted parents, but we get the job done just the same. For example, nappy changing without sight will involve getting our hands pretty mucky, as we check to make sure we have cleaned that little bottom thoroughly. By the way, many VI parents find it helpful to dry that bottom with tissue, before starting to wash with water, so they are clear which liquid they are dealing with!

Recently I had a mum in one of my classes who was worried she wouldn't be able to bathe her baby in the way that was recommended, because she'd been taught she must hold him with her right arm, and wash him with her left, but being right-handed, she felt unable to do things that way around, with her 'seeing hand' tied up supporting a slippery baby! It struck me that the midwife explaining bathing hadn't been clear enough that there isn't one fixed way we must wash a newborn, and that she was just passing on her personal way of doing it as a guide.

Making up formula feeds, too, is something which can be done safely by VI parents, with some adaptions. Parents with a little useful vision may find it useful to measure out boiled water into a jug with large, clear markings, before decanting into the bottle and adding powder. For those with no sight, the most accurate way to measure water for formula is to use talking kitchen scales: (1 fluid ounce of water equals 1 ounce on the scales). Measuring like this is likely to take longer, particularly at first, but with care and practice can be done perfectly safely.

Breastfeeding with a visual impairment...
...It's perfectly possible, plenty of us do it!

Many people, including VI parents, worry that breastfeeding will be difficult or impossible. It is true that breastfeeding can pose some specific challenges for VI mums, but these can be overcome, given the right support, encouragement and sometimes some experienced help.

Antenatal breastfeeding classes tend to be taught in quite a visual way, and obviously VI parents can't take advantage of watching DVD clips and looking at pictures and diagrams to learn about how to position their baby and ensure he/she is latched on well to feed. Once the baby arrives, if problems arise, midwives and breastfeeding helpers may feel ill-equipped to assist a VI mum, because of lack of experience, or assumptions that successful breastfeeding requires good sight.

What you need to remember is that breastfeeding need not be a visual skill; it is so much more than that, and involves all the senses. Instead of using visual clues to check their baby's latch is good, mums need to really tune in to their baby and their own body as well. With practice, we can hear when a baby is feeding effectively, when they are 'comfort sucking', when they have stopped drinking and are dozing. Once a mum has experienced a 'good latch', with her baby drinking happily without discomfort, she will be able to recognise that sensation next time, with no need for checking how much areola is visible or other visual clues.

If supporting a VI breastfeeding mum, you will need to explain things verbally very clearly. It is often helpful to be more 'hands on' than you would normally be, as well, with the mum's permission of course. Be aware that VI mums may need to experiment to find a position that suits them, which may not be the classic 'cross-cradle hold' so often recommended in antenatal classes and maternity units. What a VI mum will need is to use one hand to feel her baby's face and line up with her breast. Positions that don't leave a hand free will mean she is really stabbing in the dark as she attempts to get that baby's mouth in the right place to start a feed! Allowing the baby to 'self-attach' and start the feed spontaneously can be particularly helpful, because this approach avoids the pressure to line up the baby and grab the perfect moment to 'get them latched on' while that little mouth is wide open. It can also help mums to realise that their baby is an active participant in the breastfeeding relationship. With practice, mum and baby will both become expert at latching on for a feed.

Of course, some VI mums experience no problems at all establishing breastfeeding, but where problems persist, it's important to get experienced help from somebody confident to support a VI mum. If you feel you don't have the skills or know-how yourself, you can help the mum to find a support person who is better equipped to support her in this area. Remind her that visual impairment needn't be a barrier to breastfeeding; it's easy to have your confidence undermined at this vulnerable time. If a health professional tells her she mustn't touch her baby's face while feeding, tell her this is nonsense! Encourage her to seek support from a breastfeeding counsellor or lactation consultant; if the first one she speaks to is negative or uncertain how to help, try somebody else. Blind Mums Connect can put mums in touch with VI peer supporters to provide encouragement and specialist information.*

Getting Out And About Is Crucial

Getting out for some fresh air, a change of scene and some social contact is vital for the mental health of all new parents and this is no less the case for VI parents. It can feel pretty overwhelming, however, for a first-time parent who is VI to tackle getting out and about on their own with their new baby. Even if we have been navigating our local area or commute to work confidently beforehand, our baby's arrival brings a new dimension, as we figure out the logistics of transporting them and keeping us both safe and comfortable as we go.

Friends and family can play an important role in encouraging VI parents to get out and about, and to build up their confidence as quickly as possible, as they become more used to going out solo with their little one. Obviously, parents will know themselves what they are comfortable with and what is necessary in terms of independent outings. What we are prepared to do will depend partly on what we did before our baby was born. But having a new baby to soothe to sleep and playgroups to go to can be a good motivation for gaining new skills or re-discovering lost confidence in this area of our lives.

If parents feel nervous, offer to keep them company to the shops, or to a coffee group, while they get used to the new demands of navigating and transporting their precious cargo. Guidedog owners can get assistance from their local training team, which may be particularly useful if they use a buggy, while the dog adjusts to this new way of working. If the first instructor they speak to is reluctant to approve them using a buggy while handling their dog, they must insist on speaking to the centre manager. Guidedogs now

---

* See www.BlindMumsConnect.org.uk

have a national policy on supporting VI parents to pull buggies, but unfortunately not all staff seem to be aware of this yet. If the parent uses a white cane, their local 'rehabilitation team' can offer support. But since confidence is the key, friends, family and doulas can often be just as valuable.

For those of us without enough sight to safely push a buggy, there is the option of using one which can be pulled along behind or beside us. Grandparents can assist by contributing to the cost of an expensive and sturdy model! An ideal buggy will have a flip-over handle, so that the baby can face forwards while being pulled, and the swivel-wheels will be at the front, so that the buggy follows easily behind the person pulling.

Baby carriers are another option, and these days they are far more readily available in many shapes, sizes and styles, to suit dads as well as mums. Since a good carrier is the nearest thing to a spare pair of hands a new parent will find, it's vital that VI parents get good information to help them choose the best one (or more!) for their individual situation. Local sling meets are a good place to compare notes with other mums, and sling libraries mean you can try before you buy. A qualified sling/babywearing consultant will be able to thoroughly explain all the options and how to use them safely, whether you want a pretty sling to use indoors while you wash up, a waterproof carrier to walk to the supermarket, or a practical alternative to hefting your buggy onto the bus!

Being a VI parent is tiring!
It's easy to forget just how tiring that newborn period can be for new parents. Lack of night-time sleep and the demands of a new routine and responsibilities can really take their toll on the best of us. For VI parents, however, this tiredness is likely to be even more acute. For a start, VI people use up more energy than sighted peers, doing routine tasks on an ordinary, pre-baby day. Navigating to work, shopping, cooking, doing housework, making coffee, cooking, all require from us more skills and a higher level of thought and concentration. Caring for a new baby, therefore, will inevitably be more tiring for VI parents, before we even consider how much their little darling is sleeping at night!

We should also bear in mind that when in sole charge of a baby or toddler, VI parents will have far less, if any, 'down time'. Unlike our fully-sighted peers, we don't have the option of watching our baby rolling on a rug while we sit on the sofa with a smart phone or a magazine. 'Watching' our little one will involve being close beside them or actually touching them, in order to keep track of their reactions, movements and games. Arguably, this does mean that VI parents are providing a high level of very attentive parenting and interaction, which must surely benefit our children. It does, however, also mean that childcare is even more demanding for us.

Just being aware of these issues, and acknowledging the grand job they're doing can be helpful, whilst avoiding well-meant comments such as 'all mums feel that tired'. Friends, family and doulas might also help by taking care of the baby while mums have a daytime nap, and assisting with household chores and shopping trips, allowing parents to focus on their baby's care and resting where possible. As babies become more active, spending some time keeping parents company while they watch their little one playing may also be very much appreciated.

Peer support can make all the difference
Many VI parents may not have many VI friends, or at least not with children. Parenthood is a time, though, when many of us seek to connect with other people in a similar situation, for reassurance and practical advice. This is the motivation behind the national organisation Blind Mums Connect, providing information and support to VI mums across the UK, and enabling them to link up via online forums, weekly teleconferencing groups and local get-togethers. The organisation is growing rapidly and the feedback we receive is enthusiastic. Even mums with supportive friends and families really value the opportunity to feel connected to a community of other VI mums. Being able to share experiences, practical tips and encouragement really boosts mums' confidence, as well as helping them cope with the practical challenges parenting brings us.

THANKS

I would like to thank all the families who have invited me into their homes and given me the privilege of being present at such a special time in their lives.

I would also like to thank all the doulas who have supported this work for their valuable contributions.

Huge thanks to all those who have helped in the process of refining this book, including Helene Curtis, Judy Hildebrand, Tessa Barrett, Polly Curtis, Bridget Baker, Charlotte Bennie, Amba Wade, Mia Marzouk, Adele Stockton, Maddie McMahon, Mars Lord, Linda Chamberlain and Anja K-Metzner, as well as my editor Susan Last and illustrator Belinda Evans. A huge thanks to Maddie McMahon for her great contribution to the breastfeeding chapter.

A special thank you to my husband, Ron, for his infinite patience and skill in helping me with all things technical.

Finally, of course, grateful thanks to my wonderful family and friends for their constant love, support and encouragement.

REFERENCES

Clune, J. (2006) *The Triplet Diaries* Pan Books

Evans, K. (2009) *The Food of Love*, Myriad Editions

Katharina, D. (1980) *Depression after Childbirth*, Oxford University Press

Gerhardt, S. (2011) *Why Love Matters*, Routledge

Giles, F. (2003) *Fresh Milk*, Simon and Schuster

Gurevich, R. (2003) *The Doula Advantage*, Three Rivers Press

Hogg, T (2005) *Top Tips from the Baby Whisperer: Sleep* Vermillion

Karp, H.(2002) *Baby Bliss*, Penguin

Kitzinger, S. (1992) *Ourselves as Mothers*, Doubleday

Kitzinger, S. (1992) *Understanding Your Crying Baby*, 1992

La Leche League International (2010) *The Womanly Art of Breastfeeding*, Pinter & Martin

Martyn, E. (2011), *Baby Shock*, Vermilion

Murray, L. and Andrews, L. *The Social Baby*, CP Publishing

Murkoff, H., Eisenberg, A. and Hathaway, S. (2004) *What to Expect the First Year*, Simon and Schuster

Pantley, E. (2002) *The No-Cry Sleep Solution*, McGraw Hill

Raphael, D. (1977) *The Tender Gift: Breastfeeding*, Schocken Books

Romm, A. (2002) *Natural Health after Birth*, Healing Arts Press

Sears, W., Sears, R., Sears, J. and Sears, M. (2004) *The Premature Baby Book*, Little, Brown

Smith, J. (2008) *The Blokes' Guide to Babies*, Hay House

Smith, Hollie (2009) *Baby's First Year*, Headline

Stadlen, N. (2004) *What Mothers Do*, Tarcher Penguin

Stockler, B. (2003) *I Sleep at Red Lights*, St Martin's Griffin

CREDITS

The following images are reproduced by kind permission:
Photographs on pages 42, 43, 67, 69, 71, 75, 77, 80, 103, 143 by the author
Photograph on page 44 © Shellie Poulter, cranial osteopath
Photograph on page 63 © Tessa Barratt 2010
Illustration on page 73 Another baby © Anita Klein
Photographs on pages 82, 97, 100 © Karina Kaufman
Photographs on pages 95, 99 © by Lauren Leighton
All other illustrations © 2014 Belinda Evans

The following quotes are reproduced by kind permission:
Sheila Kitzinger on p. 25, 34; Kate Evans on p. 48; Emma Mahony on p. 99; Naomi Stadlen on p.142

INDΣX

Recipes from the Appendix on pages 157-165 are in italics.